# Our Debt to Greece and Rome

EDITORS

GEORGE DEPUE HADZSITS, PH.D.
*University of Pennsylvania*

DAVID MOORE ROBINSON, PH.D., LL.D.
*The Johns Hopkins University*

# VIRGIL AND HIS MEANING TO THE WORLD OF TO-DAY

BY

J. W. MACKAIL

*Honorary Fellow of Balliol College and formerly Professor of Poetry in the University of Oxford*

LONGMANS, GREEN AND CO.

55 FIFTH AVENUE

NEW YORK

1930

MACKAIL

VIRGIL



First Edition November 1922
Reprinted April 1923, May 1927
August 1930

THE PLIMPTON PRESS · NORWOOD · MASSACHUSETTS
PRINTED IN THE UNITED STATES OF AMERICA

## EDITORS' PREFACE

PROFESSOR MACKAIL has not devoted his whole book to the details of the influence of Virgil upon life and letters. That influence has been analyzed by competent hands before and repetition would be gratuitous. But, rather, he has presented us with a study of *the significance of Virgil* to the twentieth century. Others have traced the reactions of different ages to the Roman poet, with all of the varieties of different kinds of appreciation and interpretation, and much of this is implicit in Professor Mackail's judgments. The estimates of the eighteenth and nineteenth centuries enter into the truth of our determination of Virgil's meaning to the present. The remarkable similarity between our own times and the days of the Roman poet should assist us to interpret, more vividly, Virgil's message to the world, — a message that lives with spirit and power for us at the present moment.

The luminous, central idea of Virgil's life and

work concerns us here. It reveals to us a Virgil not merely historian or poet of an actual or an idealized Rome of long ago, but a Virgil, the interpreter of the abiding significance of Rome and Italy. Where does the permanence of the Aeneid lie? A fine critic of Virgil has said: Aeneas is " an ideal and mystical figure standing outside time and place, that seems to be now Aeneas, now Rome, now the soul of Man setting forth doubtfully on the pilgrimage of a dimly descried eternal glory."

To every age does this vision belong. It will continue to have importance for future aspiration. Virgil is one of those personalities that Nature creates in only her most amazing moods, when she wills to give to the world heroic figures of commanding grace or thought to lead the race to higher levels.

Revolt against the past should not include rebellion against what is eternally good and true. Professor Mackail's book is offered as a contribution to the highly important question of our debt to Virgil. This volume is the fourth to appear in the series, known as " Our Debt to Greece and Rome." Its eloquence amply meets the aims and purposes of the Library as a whole to trace the influence and clarify the significance of Greek and Roman thought and culture in their relation to our own time. The artist in Virgil and the human element in Virgil belong at once to the Old and to the New.

# CONTENTS


| CHAPTER | | PAGE |
|---|---|---|
| I. | The Divine Poet: the Interpreter of Life for All Time | 3 |
| II. | Virgil's World: Its Meaning for and Its Likeness to Our Own World . . . . . . . . . . . | 11 |
| III. | Virgil's Predecessors: Or, a Study in the Evolution of Poetry . . . . . . . . . . . | 22 |
| IV. | Life of Virgil: as the Background of His Work and as an Example to Poets . . . . | 29 |
| V. | The Eclogues and the New Humanism: Their Influence on European Poetry; the Vergiliana. . . . . . . . . . | 45 |
| VI. | The Georgics: Life at Peace; Their Influence and Their Importance, To-day . . . . . | 59 |
| VII. | Concentration on the Epic . . | 72 |
| VIII. | The Structure of the Aeneid, as a Masterpiece of Design and Execution. . . . . . . . | 86 |

CONTENTS

CHAPTER PAGE

IX. The Human Element, Permanent and Vital . . . . . . . 100

X. The Italo-Roman Ideal, Created by Virgil and Continuing to Our Own Day, as the Hope of the World . . . . . . . . . . 111

XI. Virgil in the Medieval and Modern World . . . . . . . 120

XII. Style and Diction: the Virgilian Hexameter . . . . . . 142

Notes . . . . . . . . . . . . . . 153

Bibliography . . . . . . . . . . 158

Contributors to the Fund . . . 161

# VIRGIL AND HIS MEANING TO THE WORLD OF TO-DAY

# VIRGIL
## AND HIS MEANING TO THE WORLD OF TO-DAY

### I. THE DIVINE POET

POETRY is, technically, human speech wrought by art into musical utterance; vitally, it is the interpretation of life in its highest terms. The progress or process of poetry is its movement through the ages, not only from poet to poet, but from country to country, from race to race, from language to language. In each, it is the expression, in patterns of words, of the instinct and effort of mankind to discover, to disengage, and to fix the essential truth and beauty which underlie the confused appearances of life. Its function is, in the words of Shelley, " to lift the veil from the hidden beauty of the world, and make familiar objects be as if they were not familiar ": or, in the equally penetrating phrase of a living poet, " to condense out of the flying vapours of the world an image of perfection."

Latin poetry is one of the great incarnations of this endless world-movement; and Virgil as the greatest of Latin poets holds a conspicuous place in the line of its torch-bearers. Before entering on a study of Virgil, before attempting to portray and appreciate his work and its meaning to us, it will be well to point out, in brief summary, the importance of Latin poetry for an age separated from it so far as ours is, its relation to the actual life of the present day, and its relevance to the structure of modern civilization as well as to our artistic or literary sense. If this is once established, the claim which Virgil has on our attention will be seen as larger and higher than we had realized; though it would be sufficient ground for such a claim that he is, by general and indeed universal consent, one of the five or six chief poets of the world. For the place of these poets is secure and indefeasible. Supreme works of art, while the product of a particular age and country and the flower of a civilization which is itself transitory, are the inheritance of the human race. They are immortal in so far as immortality can be ascribed to anything created by man.

But the importance for the present age of

the masterpieces of Latin literature rests also on special grounds. It is not only that Virgil and Horace, Cicero and Livy, are "classics" in the proper and authentic sense of that word; that their writings are of an excellence unsurpassed and in some respects unequalled by anything that we have to set beside them whether from the product of our own day or from that of the intervening centuries; that they present to us at once a standard, a model, and a stimulus for our own highest efforts; and that they embody ideals which are as living and as fertile now as they were two thousand years ago. This might conceivably be true of works produced by a race and a civilization quite alien from our own. But the Latin classics are in the direct line of our own ancestry. Rome is our mother, Latin our second mother-tongue. Not only is the civilization of Europe and America based on Roman foundations; not only have our machinery of government, our municipal institutions, our jurisprudence and our theology, their roots in Rome; but the language which we use daily as the instrument of thought and the vehicle of expression has been moulded by Latin influence. While this is more obvious among the Latin races, — for the name there sufficiently emphasizes the fact — yet it is hardly less true of the English-speaking world. Latin is not, in the strict sense, a foreign language to us; it is a vital constructive element of the first importance in our own.

This is true of our whole literature, both prose and poetry, but of poetry very particularly. There are of course collateral sources, as well as our own native springs. The early Scandinavian and Teutonic poetry owed nothing to Latin; nor did that of the Arabs and the kindred Semitic races. We have in modern times become acquainted with another foreign world in the poetry of the Far East, which seems likely to have a marked influence on the development of Western thought and art. But it remains substantially accurate to say, as was said by Gray in the eighteenth century, that "the descent," or movement, "of poetry has been from Greece to Italy, and from Italy to England." In that single sentence he laid the foundation, and gave the guiding line, for an historical and scientific study of English poetry. Greece reached us in the first instance through Rome, and as interpreted — one might almost say, as Europeanized — by the Latin mind. But the Latin mind itself was not only interpretative, it was creative. Virgil is not merely a prince of poets; he is one of the makers and founders of English poetry. He has exercised, and continues to exercise, this influence both directly and by indirect transmission. The influence has been continuous, from Bede and Cynewulf in the eighth century down to poets who are writing now. Virgil is one of the few Latin classics who were never lost sight of even in the Dark Ages. He has always been a schoolbook for youth, a treasure-house for mature appreciation, a model for artists. He is a "lord of language," as Tennyson truly says of him, who stands out as having shewn what perfect expression is, as having achieved the utmost beauty, melody, and significance, of which human words seem to be capable. He has given expression, once for all, to many of our highest thoughts and most profound emotions. Nor has he, like others who in their day have been great germinal forces, become absorbed in or been replaced by his successors. For he is a consummate artist; and a work of art is substantive and permanent in its value. It is not a means to an end, but an end attained. Homer, Virgil, Shakespeare remain alive after hundreds or thousands of years.

They retain their uplifting and enlarging influence; they speak directly to us and interpret actual life to us as much as ever. They have not a mere historical value or a mere antiquarian interest. To each generation, to each individual reader, they come afresh as revelations of the beauty of the world and the wonder of the human soul. " Creations " in the full sense of that word, they are " lordly as at the first day." Indeed it may be said of the masterpieces of poetry that they actually grow in vitality and significance with the process of time, as they absorb and incorporate into themselves an added volume of intermediate imagination and experience. For they come to us now not only with their original and imperishable virtue, but with the accumulated associations of all the ages through which they have passed. They are at once set in perspective by distance and enriched by history; they are something new and something different. They are not wholly new, even when we come on them for the first time, because much of their content has been unconsciously inherited by us, or has reached us indirectly through intermediate channels. When we make acquaintance with them, it is a recognition as well as a discovery. But they are not outworn. It is no paradox to say that they may actually mean more to each successive age. Our appreciation of them, it may be urged, must be incomplete, because we cannot place ourselves at the poet's point of view, because we cannot regain his environment, or live in the world in which he lived and which in his poetry he interpreted and transfigured. This is true; but against the loss — for loss there is — has to be set a real gain. The colours tone rather than fade; the outlines are not blurred so much as softened. The sharp freshness of the work as it first reached the world new from the artist's hand has turned into a mellow glow. The structural lines of the composition come out more significantly. Beauties and subtleties are seen which to a contemporary reader were invisible, and of which even the artist himself may not have been articulately conscious. The masterpiece places itself with a background and a foreground. It becomes for us not a mere detached work of art which has been preserved from the past, but a focus of the multiplex human movement, a lamp whose rays stream out over the whole integrated fabric of human life. In a very real sense, it is possible for us to appreciate Shakespeare more, to understand him better, than he was appreciated and understood by his Elizabethan audiences, for whom he was only one among many other popular dramatists. So likewise is it possible for us to appreciate Virgil more, though he was for them "the divine poet," than he was appreciated by those who "spoke Latin at Rome" in the Augustan Empire.

## II. VIRGIL'S WORLD

PERIODS of marked character and significance in the history of national culture or of international civilization have often been, by a convenient custom, singled out and denoted by a name. That name may be only a conventional label; or it may be the name of some individual, a ruler or a thinker or an artist, in whom the whole movement of the time appears to be concentrated more or less fully. The Elizabethan Age, the Age of Louis XIV, the Napoleonic Age, the Victorian Age are instances of terms of general acceptance. While they may not bear any rigorous analysis, they are not only useful for the sake of brevity, but relevant to a large comprehension of the epochs which they denote. But almost as frequent, and equally useful, are those terms which mark an age by the name of some one in whom its intellectual or spiritual life reached its highest expression and exercised its most definite influence on the world. The ages of Phidias and of Plato in Greece, of Aquinas,

Dante, Petrarch in the Middle Ages, of Raphael and Michael Angelo in the later Renaissance, of Shakespeare and Milton, Newton and Darwin in the annals of England, have this kind of claim for recognition, and have been recognized accordingly. There are those who would substitute for the names of the Elizabethan and Victorian Ages those of the Age of Shakespeare and the Age of Tennyson.

In Roman history — and Roman history is, for a time extending over some six or seven hundred years, the history of the civilized world — there are several periods of special importance. The most important of all is that which witnessed the downfall of the Republic and the foundation of the Empire. It was then that the political and civil organization was created under which the European world lived for more than a thousand years, and on which its subsequent developments have been mainly founded. It was then that the problem of a world-empire based on law, preserving liberty, and securing peace was for the first time faced, and a provisional solution found for it. It was then also that the literary genius of the Latin race culminated in the works of the greatest Roman historians, orators and poets; and that the Latin language was moulded into forms which have ever since been a common heritage and a permanent model for mankind.

This period, while any definite date for its beginning and end is of course quite arbitrary, may be taken for ordinary purposes as covering between fifty and sixty years of the first century before the Christian Era. It coincides pretty nearly with the life of Virgil. To understand Virgil, to read him with due appreciation, one must realize not only that he was a great artist, but that he stands in a very special relation to the whole import of an age which was one of the main turning-points in history. Not only is he the foremost figure in a group of writers in whom the Latin language as a vehicle of thought and emotion reached its highest point. He also combines in himself, in an unique way and to an unique extent, the racial and cultural elements out of which the Latin civilization was compounded. He was the chief exponent and interpreter, in the forms of creative art, of the aims and ideals of his age in the evolution and government of human life. He looked, as few have done, before and after. Standing as he did at the point of junction between two worlds, he gave expression to the past of his nation and race, and he anticipated, he even in a sense created, their future. In his hands Italy and Rome became sacred names, and his own name became inseparably linked with theirs. He was, in the simple and striking phrase which became current in the century after his death, *Romanus Vergilius*, " Roman Virgil." He was from the first the prophet of the Roman Empire; and he was accepted later as the precursor or herald of the spiritual Rome in which the divine will was to be accomplished and the divine order made manifest to the world. He fixed for the imagination of the Roman race, and of the nations which it subdued or incorporated, the limit of its aspiration and achievement, the very sea-mark of its utmost sail. When he had finished his work, and not until then, according to the belief of the early Church, the time was come for the incarnation of Christ. The establishment of peace under an universal empire was the prelude to the appearance of the Prince of Peace. It was recorded and glorified by the Augustan historians and poets. Among them, Virgil is the central figure; and the Augustan Age may be called also, and called appropriately, the Age of Virgil.

It is accordingly desirable, it is even necessary, towards intelligent study of Virgil and towards any adequate appreciation of his genius and of its meaning to us, to get some general view of the age in which he lived and the world which he interpreted, no less than of the earlier history of Latin poetry in the hands of his predecessors. For both purposes, a rapid glance must be taken over past history. The relevance of the points mentioned in this summary will become clear when we pass on to a sketch of Virgil's own life and work, and to consideration of the dominant motives in his poetry.

The Roman Republic, originally a small city-state with a population of farmers and tradesmen occupying a territory of a few miles square on the lower Tiber, had early in its history developed a singular genius for war and colonization, for municipal organization and commerce. By the beginning of the third century B.C. it held a dominant position in central Italy, not only among the Umbro-Latin communities of which it was one, but more widely throughout the territory inhabited by the kindred stocks of Sabellians and Oscans. By the decay of the once great Etruscan League it had been brought into direct contact with the Celtic peoples who then occupied the Po valley and the Lombard plain. At the other end of the Italian peninsula it had come into close relations, whether peaceable or hostile, with the Greek or semi-Grecized states of Southern Italy and Sicily. These relations, alike in commerce and in politics, were necessarily extended further. Sicily was the strategic centre of the Western Mediterranean, and was in joint Greek and Carthaginian occupation. Its control was vital to any Power which sought expansion in those seas and in the circle of surrounding countries, Italy, Southern Gaul, Spain and Northern Africa.

Rome and Carthage became rivals for that control, and for the commercial and political predominance which it carried. The armed conflict between them lasted, with intervals, for more than a hundred years, and was only ended by the total destruction of Carthage. The Second Punic War, a desperate struggle of seventeen years during which Rome was brought to the brink of ruin by the genius of the Carthaginian general Hannibal, left indelible traces on the Roman imagination, no less than on the course of Rome's subsequent history. She emerged from the contest mistress of Italy, and a world-power; but also with a loss, never wholly repaired, of her older and nobler traditions, of simplicity, patriotism, a high standard of honour, all that was meant by Roman virtue. The poison of wealth, the greed for exploitation of subject countries, the craving for idle amusement and the excitements of town life, crept into all classes of the community. The century which passed between the destruction of Carthage and the dictatorship of Julius Caesar is a record of immense material and territorial expansion, of corrupt and increasingly incapable government, of domestic dissensions and sanguinary civil wars. The huge monarchies of the Near East, founded by the marshals of Alexander the Great in the provinces of his gigantic empire, were crumbling to pieces, and one after another fell by conquest, or lapsed as derelict, into Roman control, as those of India passed under English rule in the century between the battle of Plassey and the annexation of the Punjab. The kingdoms of Macedonia, Asia, Syria, became Roman provinces; Egypt became a Roman protectorate. The vassal monarchies of the Asiatic frontier, fragments of the enormous Seleucid empire, followed suit. The whole Mediterranean was turned into a Roman lake. The new Oriental provinces were the richest, the most populous and the most highly civilized part of this enlarged dominion. The fatal lure of the East began to work. The ghost of Alexander's empire, which had stretched from the Adriatic to the Indus, from Bactria to the Sudan, kept rising from the grave to vex and dazzle the imagination of the West. The Asiatic policy of Rome, like her Asiatic frontier, was in perpetual fluctuation. In Virgil's seventeenth year, a great Roman army, led out across the Euphrates on a mad adventure of mixed conquest and plunder, was utterly destroyed by the Parthians in the Mesopotamian desert.

All the while, things had been going badly at home. Roman control of Italy became more and more oppressive. The Italian peoples, held down by a splendid system of military roads and a network of garrisoned Roman colonies, were treated not as allies but as subjects. But under this pressure there arose the feeling of joint Italian nationality. It shewed itself on both sides; at Rome, by a movement towards incorporation of Italy in the Roman Republic; in Italy, by a movement to shake off the Roman yoke and create an Italian nation out of the complex aggregation of tribes, communities and municipalities which filled the peninsula. After smouldering for many years, the fire blazed up on the assassination of the Roman tribune who had brought forward legislative proposals for remodelling the constitution and extending Roman citizenship to all the allies. The Social War broke out. An Italian government was set up, and a new capital founded in the centre of the peninsula. The immediate object of the revolt failed; Roman arms conquered, after three years of desperate fighting. But in the course of the war or immediately after it, Roman citizenship was given to all Italy south of the Po. The status of the north remained long anomalous; it was not until 42 B.C., the year of the battle of Philippi, that Cisalpina, the whole region between the Alps and the Apennines, ceased to be technically a province. It was in that region that Livy, the creator for all time of the Roman legend, and Virgil, the prophet and poet both of unified Italy and of imperial Rome, were born.

Hardly had the pacification of Italy been accomplished, when intestine struggles came to a head in the Roman Commonwealth itself. Half a century of revolutions, proscriptions, and furious civil wars brought the State, and European civilization with it, to the breaking point and almost to destruction. Events crowded thick on one another; there was no time to take breath, no opportunity to recover solvency. In swift succession came the revolutionary legislation of 88 B.C.; Sulla's march on Rome, and its occupation for the first time in history by a Roman army; the Marian reign of terror; the return of the Asiatic legions and the battle of the Colline Gate; Sulla's dictatorship and massacres; civil war spreading in the provinces, and the revolt of Spain; the great slave-insurrection in Italy; pirate-fleets filling the Mediterranean; the abortive revolutionary movement of Catiline; the total bankruptcy of government and the patchwork of the first triumvirate; its collapse, and Caesar's descent into Italy with his veteran army; the world-wide Civil War of 49–45 B.C., ending with Caesar's complete victory and the establishment, under the name of a dictatorship for ten years (like the ten-years' Consulate of Napoleon in 1799), of a virtual monarchy; his assassination, which plunged the broken world into complete chaos; fresh civil wars conducted by gigantic armies; the second triumvirate and the extinction of the senatorial party as an organized force; the provisional partition of the Roman world into an Eastern and a Western dominion; the long duel for empire between Octavian and Antony, determined at last by the battle of Actium: and then the forty-five years' principate of Augustus. "The Empire is peace" was the motto of the new government. It set itself slowly and steadily to restore order, to liquidate debt, to fix and guard the frontiers, to revive agriculture, to organize administration, to reinstate religion and purify morals. The Roman world had been racked and was bleeding to death; the Roman virtue had nearly perished; there was a great material and moral bankruptcy. The task was to save all that was possible out of the general wreckage. Yet hope was not lost. A new generation was growing up. Spirit, energy and genius survived. Men's minds were ready to turn from the past as from a horrible nightmare, to apply their whole energies to reconstruction, and even to hail, in the *Pax Augusta,* the dawn of a new Golden Age.

## III. VIRGIL'S PREDECESSORS

WHAT, during that period, had been the course and aim of Latin poetry? Its history had effectively begun with the entry of Greek influence. "The descent of poetry," in Gray's words already cited, "was from Greece to Italy." That influence began to manifest itself in the interval between the first and second Punic Wars, a time of victorious and many-sided expansion in which Rome became fully conscious of her own greatness, and set to equip herself fully as a civilized Power of the first rank. Up till then, Latin poetry had consisted of rude ballads and hymns, hardly amounting to what could be called a literature. That had served for domestic use. It was not sufficient for the prestige and expression of an expanding State. Rome put herself to school. An educated class formed itself. The instinct for creative expression was awakened. Systematic efforts were made to enter into the sphere of Hellenistic culture. The Greek language was taught and learned; the

Greek poets, both the classics and the moderns, were read, studied, imitated. Translations of Greek masterpieces were assiduously made. In these, as also in original poetical works, the traditional Latin rhythms and metres were soon displaced by a foreign metrical system based on strict numerical laws. In both cases the old native forms became submerged. They survived in popular usage; and they were so inseparable from the structure of the language as to make the Latin hexameter, for instance, something organically different from the Greek hexameter, with a rhythm and colour of its own. But otherwise they disappeared from the main current of national poetry.

It took a hundred and fifty years or so to complete the revolution effectively, and to mould the stubborn Latin language fully into the new forms. A single generation carried the first positions with a rush; then came a long time of slow patient advance; then a second rapid movement completed the conquest.

Three distinct forms of poetry, the epic, lyric and dramatic, had in Greece proper been created, carried to perfection, and given the names which they still retain. To the sphere which they included, a large extension had been given by the newer poetical impulse of the Hellenistic, or, as it is generally termed, the Alexandrian School. On the old lines, all had been already done that was possible. The new poets addressed themselves to the task of reconnecting poetry with actual life and modern interests. The old intense civic life of the free Greek States had ceased. The new age was one of large monarchies, despotically ruled, guarded by professional armies, and maintained by international trade and commerce. The interests of life were wider and also shallower. Pure and applied science had become an engrossing pursuit. Scientific agriculture was developed, and sources of wealth systematically exploited. Past history became a field of endless investigation. With kindled interest in the past came a new way of regarding the present. Three things arose, all of a capital importance towards the movement of poetry: the sense of romance, the longing for a return to nature, and the fascination of scholarship. Poetry, while it did not cease to be an interpretation of life, was a refuge from, rather than a motive force in, the actual world. Technique became a matter of intense study. Its application to the new subject-matter created by the new motives which had sprung up was equally so. Pastoral poetry, the reaction of a tired civilization from the crowd and glare and din of cities to the fresh beauty and innocent simplicity of the country, flowered forth in Sicily. Romance, substituting a new world of love and adventure for the nobler but more austere epic treatment of the mundane spectacle, was launched, in the face of jealous opposition, by the genius of Apollonius the Rhodian. Elegiac verse, already a maid-of-all-work for minor poetry, was carried to further uses by adroit and inventive handling. The so-called didactic poem — an unfortunate and rather misleading title — was an even more courageous attempt to bring the whole field of the arts and sciences within the scope of imaginative treatment and to crystallize knowledge in poetical forms. Such were the last gifts of Greek poetical genius to the world, the new paths it opened, before the Muses turned their faces westward, where their light rekindled on the virgin soil of Italy in a new language and race.

The Latin language, fertilized and enriched by Greek influence, spread in the wake of Roman conquest and expansion. Before Virgil's time it had become the common speech, at least of the educated classes, throughout Italy, and was spreading fast in the Western provinces. The other Italian languages, without cultural centres and failing to respond to the intellectual movement of the age, sank into mere provincial dialects. The development of Latin poetry was accelerated both by the swift growth of a lettered class at Rome and by the fresh blood supplied by the Romanized races.

Most of the earlier Latin poets — as indeed most of the later ones also — were themselves not Latin. Ennius, who rose so far above his predecessors that he may be called the creator of Roman epic and of Roman tragedy, was a Calabrian. Accius, the last and greatest of the Latin tragedians, two generations later, was an Umbrian, of the Adriatic coast. Plautus was also an Umbrian. Terence, the first Latin poet by whom the language was used with complete ease and grace, and with a Greek perfection of finish, was actually a Carthaginian who came to Rome as a boy slave. The assimilating power of Rome is nowhere more marked than in the field of letters. Even later, in the age of Cicero, Lucretius is the single poet of the first rank who was a Roman of the pure stock.[1]

Catullus, like Virgil himself, came from the Cisalpine province. But all alike felt themselves and would have called themselves Romans. All of them lived and wrote at Rome. With the decay of genius in the fading Hellenistic kingdoms, the shifting of the centre of gravity of the Mediterranean civilization, and the growth in the western capital of education, study, and keen literary interest, Rome became the intellectual centre of the world. The times of which a brief sketch has already been given were as stimulating and exciting as they were crowded and tragic in events. Life was lived at the highest pressure. The development of poetry in that rich soil and electric atmosphere was very swift, the product very great. The problems of technique were one after another faced and solved. Latin, in poetry as well as in prose, became within the compass of a single lifetime a language in which one could say anything, and say it with unequalled force and precision. The conquest of the Latin hexameter had been effected by the genius of Lucretius. It still remained to complete for Latin poetry what he had begun. It still remained to give it a further delicacy and melodiousness, a more exquisite movement, a higher felicity; to make it the vehicle of a fuller humanity, to create in it an interpretation of the past and an inspiration for the future. It still remained to render it, in the largest sense, the voice of Rome, of Italy, of mankind. The times were ripe for Virgil to appear.

## IV. LIFE OF VIRGIL

VIRGIL was born on the 15th October, B.C. 70, in the commune of Andes, which was somewhere in the territory attached to Mantua, then a small and comparatively unimportant provincial town. The precise situation of Andes is unknown. Its traditional identification with the hamlet of Pietola some three miles to the southeast of Mantua, though of long standing, and mentioned incidentally by Dante in the *Purgatorio* as an accepted belief, is inconsistent with the details given in the early life of Virgil by Probus the Grammarian, and with what little can be gathered or inferred from the allusions or descriptive touches in Virgil's own early poems.

His father is said to have been originally a servant, who throve in life by character and industry, and, like the father of Keats, married his employer's daughter and heiress. He settled down as a thriving yeoman-farmer, making a living particularly out of forestry and bee-keeping. Of Virgil's mother, Magia Polla, nothing is known beyond the name. It is of interest, because long afterwards it became distorted into a mystical significance, as though it indicated possession of magical powers: and that baseless belief contributed largely towards the growth of the widespread and long-continued medieval tradition of Virgil, as himself a magician and miracle-worker, or even, like the Merlin of the Arthurian legend, an enchanter born of a maiden mother and occupying a position towards the Emperor Augustus like that of Merlin towards Arthur.

Whether Virgil was a Roman citizen by birth is uncertain. It is quite probable that his father, as a substantial freeholder who may very well have held small local magistracies, had obtained the citizenship before Virgil's birth. In any case the whole family would automatically come under the general extension of full citizenship to the Cisalpine province by Julius Caesar. Modern scholars have pleased themselves by fancying that Caesar himself, in the winter progresses through the Cisalpine proconsulate which intervened between his campaigns in Transalpine Gaul, may have received Virgil's father at an interview, and that Virgil himself may have seen him and been spoken to by him, whether at Mantua, at Cremona, where he received his earlier education, or later when he was continuing it in the larger and better-equipped schools at Milan. Through some such chance meeting, it has been suggested, may have begun the acquaintance of Virgil with a boy seven years younger than himself, Caesar's orphan grandnephew and adopted heir, the future Emperor Augustus. An even more attractive fancy is that Virgil as a boy may have seen and known Catullus, whose home at Sirmio was only some five and twenty miles off. The Veronese poet's influence on the early work of Virgil is marked and profound. But it extended to the whole group of young poets to which Virgil belonged; and in any case, Catullus lived long enough — the exact date when his brief and brilliant life ended is uncertain — for Virgil to have made his personal acquaintance. Another chronological link, this time a pure coincidence, attaches Virgil's name to that of the other great poet of the Ciceronian age. Lucretius died, according to a well-authenticated tradition, on Virgil's fifteenth birthday.

Virgil's racial ancestry has been the subject of much inconclusive and perhaps somewhat idle debate. Mantua had been one of the leading cities of the old Etruscan League. The population of the town and neighbourhood was still largely of Etruscan blood. Of the Etruscan civilization and religion, both, factors of much importance in the earlier times of the Roman Republic, Virgil was certainly a diligent student. He repeatedly lays stress on the Etruscan origins of Mantua; and the tone of these passages, particularly of one in the Catalogue of the tenth book of the *Aeneid,*[2] seems one of personal pride not only in his birthplace, but in an ancient race with a great past to which he felt himself to belong. The main population of the whole of Cisalpine Gaul, however, was, as the name of the province indicates, Celtic. The names *Vergilius* and *Maro* have both been traced, on very doubtful arguments, to Celtic roots; and the romantic strain in Virgil's own temperament has, even more arbitrarily, been held by some modern critics to indicate, or even to prove, that he was of Celtic blood. Nor is this all. Macrobius,[3] at the end of the fourth century, speaks of him as a Venetian. Mantua was at no time within the district known as Venetia, though not far from its western border; and this statement accordingly must imply some further tradition of the origin of his family from a third and totally different source, the race of the Veneti, who probably came of an Illyrian stock with Slavonic affinities. But here we are wandering in realms of pure conjecture: and no doctrine or theory of racial characteristics throws much light on the origins of individual genius. That Virgil was of mixed race is at least highly probable. The mixture or coalescence of strains in him, without laying undue stress on it, may be taken as a symbol of his share in the creation of a unified Italy, not merely as a theoretic ideal but as an actual nation, which has only in our own day fully realized itself.

From the schools of Milan, which corresponded broadly to a modern provincial university, Virgil passed on at about the age of eighteen to Rome. It was the centre of advanced studies for all the Latin-speaking world, and the nursery of a brilliant group of young poets. Several of these attained high distinction. Some, like Aemilius Macer of Verona and Quintilius Varus of Cremona, came from Virgil's own neighbourhood, and were his intimate friends. His closest intimacy of all was with Cornelius Gallus, who was a native of Fréjus, a Roman colony and naval station in Narbonese Gaul. Gallus was a youth of almost exactly Virgil's own age, of great personal fascination and precocious poetical genius. Virgil and he were the two foremost members in a remarkable literary circle during the Civil Wars. They studied and wrote in conjunction. The whole group to which the two belonged originated a new poetical movement. It had a triple aim: first, a higher and more sustained technical quality than had hitherto been reached in Latin poetry; next, the assimilation and transmutation into poetical forms of the Alexandrian learning which had become the heritage of the new intellectual class at Rome; and lastly, the embodiment in these forms of the new romanticism.

Virgil's own studies, continued for many years, indeed throughout his life, were wide and assiduously pursued. He began at Rome with the normal course of rhetoric and its cognate studies in language and literature, which was the foundation of the all-important art of oratory. But he soon passed on from these to the pursuit of Greek philosophy. In the lecture-room of the Epicurean Siro he may have made his first acquaintance with the poetry of Lucretius, to which his own owes so much. In that of the rhetorician Epidius he is said (though the dates make this improbable) to have had young Octavius, afterwards the Emperor Augustus, as one of his junior fellow-students. But for some ten years at this period we know little of his life except that it was a time of slowly maturing genius and ardent study, in a circle of kindred spirits. During these years, his father had died and his mother married again. He is not known to have kept up afterwards any personal connection with the country of his birth and boyhood. He had sufficient patrimony to live the life of a scholar, to study and to travel, to devote himself wholly to letters and to philosophical and historical studies. His great shyness, a certain rusticity of manner which he retained through life, and physical health which was always delicate, combined to keep him from any attempt to launch out, as many of his circle did, on public life in a civil, administrative, or military career.

When he was nearly thirty, the course of public events almost wrecked, and then permanently secured, his material fortune. After the battle of Philippi, the first task of the victorious triumvirs was to provide for the demobilization and settlement of their immense armies. For that purpose, the lands of Italian towns or communes which had taken the other side in the Civil War were confiscated. Virgil's inheritance was included in the confiscation of the territory of Cremona and part of that of Mantua. But he had powerful and active friends. Among them, besides Gallus and Varus, who had already risen to influential positions, was Pollio, the actual administrator of that district. By their intervention, Virgil was not only compensated for the loss of his patrimony by a small landed estate in Campania, but was introduced to the intimacy of what was now becoming an Imperial Court. Prosperity and even considerable wealth were assured to him for the remainder of his life.

Soon after, in 37 B.C., he published the collection of *Eclogues* or Selected Poems, *Poesie Scelte,* also known by the name of the *Bucolics* or Pastorals. The immediate welcome given in all quarters to this small and unassuming volume will be mentioned and discussed later. It made its shy author at once famous; he found himself, to his great embarrassment, vociferously cheered if he entered the theatre. There is a story of the Sixth *Eclogue* being recited there, with great applause, by the favourite actress Cytheris, who was the mistress of Gallus and the Lycoris of the Tenth *Eclogue*. Already Virgil was marked out by expectation as the laureate of the new régime. Pollio had introduced him to Maecenas, the Home Secretary and Minister of Reconstruction (to use modern phraseology) of the national government. The lively account given by Horace, in the fifth of his first volume of *Satires*, of the journey he made (in the year 37 or 38 B.C.) from Rome to Brindisi with Maecenas, when Virgil joined the party on the way, is the only intimate glimpse of Virgil which we possess for this period, and the only sketch of him, tantalizingly slight indeed, which has reached us at first hand from the pen of an intimate friend.

It was at Maecenas' instance, and not only with his encouragement but under some pressure from him, that Virgil now undertook the composition of the *Georgics*. He was not however in any way hurried over the work. About seven years were spent on it, chiefly at his new home in Campania. He had a house at Rome, in the recently laid out fashionable quarter on the Esquiline, but seldom used it, and never for long together. His winters were spent mainly on the coast near Naples, his summers on his own estate in the lovely hill-country of the interior; it is from "sweet Parthenope," overlooking the Bay of Naples, that he dates his *Georgics* in the graceful concluding lines. But he also travelled and resided for considerable periods in the South, near Tarentum, and also in Sicily; and intimate personal knowledge of many districts in Central Italy is indicated both in the *Georgics* and more particularly in the *Aeneid*.

The *Georgics* were completed by the autumn of 29 B.C., when they were read aloud by Virgil to Octavianus at Atella after his return to Italy from settling the affairs of the Eastern provinces. They were published soon after, and placed their author beyond dispute at the head of both contemporaries and predecessors, as the foremost of Latin poets.

Virgil was now turned forty. He had from early years contemplated the writing of an Italian epic. He had never lost sight of that design; nor had he ever for long together ceased to ponder over it, to lay plans for it, and to work at it. It now began to take shape in the general scheme of the *Aeneid*. This became the task of the rest of his life. It was urged on him by the Court; it was called for by the unanimous wishes and expectations of the public; and it opened out to him the possibility of embracing in a single great masterpiece all the motives which stirred him most as a poet. It gave scope for Roman pride and Italian patriotism, for the fascination of history and archaeology, for romantic narrative, delicate psychological insight, human emotion. It enabled him to give expression to faith in the future as based on and interpreted by the past, and to his own deep thoughts on life, death, and the destiny of mankind. Absorbed in this engrossing occupation, he withdrew himself more and more from public notice and from society. If few incidents of these later years have come down to us, it is no doubt because there were few to chronicle. One has to be mentioned, because it marks a definite break in his own life, and left, as we may judge, its mark on his poetry. This was the disgrace and suicide of Gallus in 26 B.C. The two friends, once so intimate, had indeed drifted apart in the course of time and circumstance. Gallus had plunged into public life, and had risen in it with a rapidity only exceeded by the swiftness of his fall. That precocious poetical brilliance which had acted as a stimulus of immense force on Virgil's more slowly maturing and more laboriously working mind (somewhat as Coleridge in early years acted on Wordsworth), seems to have faded quite away. But the friendship had remained, if only as a sacred tradition. After its tragic ending, we can trace, or think we trace, in the survivor a new accent of wistful brooding, an added shade, beyond what advancing years by themselves would bring, upon the native melancholy of his temper.

The ground-plan of the *Aeneid* passed through many phases; its detailed construction occupied many years. As early as 25 B.C. Augustus was writing to Virgil from Spain, asking for news of its progress. It was awaited in Rome with no less eager general interest: "Something greater than the *Iliad,*" in the words used of it about the same time by Propertius,[4] who may have heard portions of it read by the author, was the widespread expectation.[5] It was two years or more later when, according to the well-known story, Virgil read three complete books aloud to Augustus and his sister Octavia. One of them was the Sixth, in the conclusion of which he had just incorporated the famous lamentation for Marcellus, Octavia's only son and the destined heir of the Empire.

Gradually the poem grew towards completion. In 19 B.C., three more years were, in Virgil's own mind, to be spent on final revision, and on the addition, throughout, of those last almost imperceptible touches by which a poet, like a painter, often kindles a whole work into new life and beauty. In the course of that summer he determined to make a prolonged tour to Greece and the coasts and islands of the Aegean, in the hope, it would seem, that change to fresh scenes would restore a vitality which he felt flagging. It was an unfortunate project. He was not strong enough to stand the fatigue and discomfort of travel. He was restless and dissatisfied. When, on reaching Athens, he found the Emperor there on his return to Italy from a progress through the Eastern provinces, he decided to go back with him. The change of plan was made too late. On a visit he made to Megara just before sailing, he contracted a low fever of malarial type. He had no strength to rally from it. On the voyage to Italy he grew steadily worse; and he died at Brindisi, a few days after landing, on the 21st of September. By annalistic reckoning he was about a month short of completing his fifty-first year: in reality, owing to the length of the "year of confusion" when Julius Caesar reformed the Calendar, his life extended over quite three months more.

On his death-bed he begged to have the manuscript of the *Aeneid* brought to him that he might burn it with his own hands. The friends who were with him of course refused to do this, but had to pacify him with some promise or half-promise that it should not be published: a promise which, if made, was fortunately for the world not kept. His ashes were taken to Naples, and buried near his seaside villa at Posilipo, where a stately tomb was erected over them.[6]

Virgil never married. A moiety of his considerable fortune was left to his half-brother, the son of Magia by her second marriage, and, as it would seem, the only surviving member of the family; the rest, in various portions, among his friends.

There are few anecdotes of him; and of these the greater number are apocryphal. Throughout life he shrank from publicity. Delicacy of health unfitted him for civic life and even for active physical exercises; and as has been already noted, he retained, in a marked slowness of speech and rusticity of appearance and habits, the traces of his peasant origin. But it is interesting to know that his reading voice — not a common thing, perhaps, among poets — was of extraordinary beauty.

Of the busts and statues which were made of him when alive and multiplied after his death, none are known to survive even in copies. Those which have at one time or another had his name attached to them are in no case authentic, and most of them bear no likeness at all to the authentic descriptions of his appearance. Purely imaginative portraits of him have been made by many great artists; by Mantegna and Botticelli and Raphael, by Blake and Burne-Jones. But in 1896 there was discovered, in excavations made at Sousse in Tunisia, a fine mosaic floor belonging to the central hall of a Roman villa. The principal panel, which was practically intact, shows Virgil seated between two Muses; he holds on his knees the roll of the *Aeneid*, open at the words *Musa mihi causas memora.* The date of this mosaic is fixed by experts as not much more than a century after Virgil's death. It is not only in itself well executed, but is clearly copied from a very fine picture, painted at a time when authentic portraits of Virgil were numerous, and when a live tradition of his appearance still survived. This portrait shews him such as he is described in his ancient biographies, and such as we can well believe him to have really been in his later years. The face is thin and worn, the complexion sallow; the delicate features bear traces of habitually poor health. The closely-cut hair is dark brown, shewing flecks of grey; the forehead finely moulded; the mouth sensitive and *souffrant;* the eyes large, deeply-set and luminous. Such as it is, this is all that we have to bring before us the bodily image of the poet of Rome.

## V. THE ECLOGUES AND THE NEW HUMANISM

VIRGIL'S genius developed slowly. He wrote with difficulty and was never satisfied with what he wrote. For many years his work was experimental, tentative, immature in accomplishment and uncertain in handling. Yet from the first it impressed his contemporaries with the sense of wonderful promise, as the new voice of a new age.

Latin poetry was at the conflux of cross-currents; its movements were perplexed, its future uncertain alike in aim and in attainment. The main effort of the writers then most recent and most popular had been to be elaborately scholarly. "Learned" was the stock epithet of praise for a poet. They concentrated on form rather than on substance, on ornament rather than on structure. Art more and more passed into artifice. They sought assiduously to reach the same standard of minute workmanship as had been established in Hellenistic poetry by the School of Alexandria. The

Alexandrian poets had been above all trained scholars and technical experts. The poet most admired and imitated at Rome was Euphorion, chief librarian at the Seleucid Court, as Callimachus, the head of the school, had been a generation earlier chief librarian at the Court of the Ptolemies. The post in both cases was not merely that of keeper of a library; it was that of President of a University. The poetry of which these two names are representative was marked by high technical finish, by ostentatious learning, and by fluctuation between dry hardness and deliquescent sentiment. Its vices, even more than its virtues, appealed strongly to Roman taste. In the poems of Catullus we see its pernicious effects gaining more and more control over his own lyrical genius. In the poetical interregnum which followed Catullus' death, Latin poetry ran the risk of losing itself completely in a desert or a morass. Pursuit of pedantic artifice in language went alongside of a lax and shallow treatment of life.

From this collapse towards which Latin poetry seemed heading, the *Eclogues* were the first open sign of recovery. They opened out a new life for it. Poetry breathed the air again.

Though not yet disentangled fully, it was no longer suffocated in the swathings of a stifling convention. The chrysalis was broken, though the wings of the butterfly still clung soft and crumpled and had not expanded into breadth and brilliance. The universal popularity and amazing success of the *Eclogues* came from the sense of this release. A new voice in poetry had made itself audible, and it was the voice of a new life. A poet had appeared, whose mastery of his art was indeed still very imperfect, whose work was timid, tentative, sometimes not only uncertain but imitative and feeble; but who already had, beyond all mistake, a grave sweetness, a tenderness and grace (the *molle atque facetum* of Horace's admirable characterization),[7] a melodiousness of language and beauty of phrasing previously unknown. The specific Virgilian charm disclosed itself. It was a new thing in the world then, and now after nearly two thousand years it has lost nothing of its potency. To each new reader, the *Eclogues* are still a revelation.

The *Eclogues* were Virgil's first published work. They are only a small fraction of what he had then written. He tells us himself that to produce an epic, "to sing of kings and battles," had been his youthful ambition; and some early work which may date back even to that period can be traced here and there in parts of the *Aeneid*. But he experimented in many poetical forms; composing, we are told, copiously, and then cutting down so mercilessly that a single line might be all that was left to shew for a whole day's labour in composition. He would not give to the world anything but the distilled product, and even that he gave with reluctance. To his own work he was, from first to last, the most fastidious and merciless of critics. He destroyed, or succeeded in suppressing, nearly all the poetry that he did not publish, the amount of which was no doubt very large. In late collections of miscellaneous Latin minor poetry there are some short pieces ascribed to him and dating, if genuine, from his early youth. The greater number are not his at all: [8] the few which may be accepted as authentic are only notable as throwing some light on his youthful studies and predilections, and giving a glimpse of the circle in which he moved. They are poetical exercises, showing little or no traces either of his distinctive manner or of his individual genius.

Even the *Eclogues* themselves Virgil seems to have published with reluctance, such as was felt in very similar circumstances by Milton when, at about the same age, and equally absorbed in intense studies over a very wide field, he gave reluctant consent to the publication of his *Ludlow Masque*. The sharp cry of annoyance which Milton then allowed to escape from him is well known. On the title page he placed a line from the *Eclogues:* [9]

Eheu! quid volui misero mihi! floribus Austrum
Perditus —

without any further words, making it abundantly clear that he regarded this public appearance, like Virgil's, premature. In both cases it was the introduction into the world not only of a new poet but of a new poetry. But the analogy does not go further; for at no period of Virgil's life, not even when in the *Aeneid* he forecasts his own immortality,[10] is there a trace of that sublime arrogance which from first to last was an element in Milton's temper. Both poets were content with nothing short of perfection. But Virgil's shrinking from publicity was genuine and excessive modesty; Milton's was intense pride; it was the feeling that what he wrote, however good, was not good enough to stand above his signature.

The ten "Eclogues," or selected poems, appeared as the manifesto of a new poetry; they were hailed as the symbol and forecast of a new age. Like the *Shepherds Calendar* of Spenser, they marked, and largely created, a whole era. Both of these small volumes were slight in content, immature in technique, loaded with imitations and struggling with worn-out conventions. Both contained a certain amount of work which was simply bad. But in both there was a new and live voice; the one inaugurated the splendours of the Augustan, the other those of the Elizabethan Age. Both, from the moment of their appearance, were recognized as landmarks in the national literature. But the *Eclogues* also exercised not only on Latin poetry, but on that of later ages and other languages, a profound and immense influence. [11]

The alternative title of the volume, the *Bucolics* or Pastorals, marks them as introducing into Western Europe a new poetical form or convention. Virgil established the Pastoral as one of the chief types of European poetry. As Sicilian and not purely Greek in origin, the pastoral is of mixed parentage; but it was in effect the last or all but the last achievement of Greek poetical invention. There had been vague earlier movements towards it, but to all intents and purposes it was the creation of Theocritus. In him also — as is the way with late products, like the art of printing — it reached full perfection at a stroke. Theocritus remains to this day the greatest, as he was the first, of the pastoral poets. But Virgil did more than transplant the pastoral from Greek to Italian soil. He gave it a new scope and a different content. We may say — and it has often been said — that he conventionalized it, though in saying this we must remember that it was from the first a highly elaborate convention and the product of a ripe, even of a decadent and partially exhausted civilization. It was an artificial though quite genuine return to nature. In Virgil's hands it becomes more complex. It hardly even makes the attempt to translate into poetry the actual life, speech and surroundings of shepherds and milkmaids. It feels after the return to nature, but the nature towards which it returns is felt and expressed not simply, but through a refracting and colouring medium of sentiment, of association, and occasionally of something approaching to mysticism. It works by enrichment rather than by simplification. Throughout these pieces, Virgil is feeling his way, not always successfully, into partly unexplored regions. Their poetical quality varies as largely as their technical accomplishment. Alongside of phrases and passages of thrilling beauty and lovely melody are others which are confused and awkward and ineffective. In some *Eclogues* he seems to limit himself to imitating in Latin the substance and cadences of his Greek masters. In several, he attempts, in a way which can hardly be called either skilful or happy, to bring contemporary events, and incidents of his own life, within the scope of the pastoral convention. He introduced into the pastoral that disastrous vein of allegory which was later the obsession of medieval poetry, and the effects of which lasted long beyond the Middle Ages. In order to appreciate what Virgil did for poetry in the *Eclogues,* we must realize that he was trying to make of it — that he did make of it when most inspired, most successful, and most himself — something wholly new. The tenth *Eclogue* is what shews most clearly what this something new was. The latest, the loveliest, and perhaps the most

Virgilian of all, it embodies the essence of romanticism, once for all, in language of exquisite melody and inimitable beauty.

In virtue of that idyl alone, Virgil takes his place as the fountain-head of romanticism for medieval and modern Europe. But for the expression of the fuller Virgilianism, as it was developed later in the *Georgics* and the *Aeneid,* the fourth *Eclogue* is the capital piece in the collection. That poem, the famous picture or prophecy of a restored Golden Age, stands quite by itself. It sounds a deeper note, and with the Virgilian sweetness incorporates a new element, the Virgilian majesty. By it he gained his unique place as the poet not of a nation only, but of the human race. Early in the history of the Church, the Child whose approaching birth he celebrates in this poem was identified with Jesus Christ. "Maro, the prophet of the Gentiles," took his place alongside of David and Isaiah, in the ranks of seers and sibyls, as a poet who had written under direct if unconscious inspiration, and to whom had been allowed the vision of God incarnate among men. That belief lasted throughout and far beyond the Middle Ages. Its effects, though not the belief itself, continue now. For Virgil is felt to be the supreme instance of the *anima naturaliter Christiana;* the articulate voice of a whole creation groaning and travailing in pain together, subject to vanity not willingly but in hope, waiting in earnest expectation for the manifestation of the Sons of God.

At this point must be mentioned three poems which at one time or another passed under Virgil's name, and are now printed, together with the scraps of juvenile verse to which reference has already been made, under the general heading of *Vergiliana,* either as a separate volume or as an appendix to complete editions of Virgil's works. All these were, beyond reasonable doubt, written in his lifetime and are products of the literary circle to which he belonged. But the problems of authorship which they raise are complex and to some extent perhaps insoluble.

The first of these, the *Ciris,* is the most interesting of the three, both from the real, though crude and undisciplined genius which it discloses and from the light it throws on the origins of Virgilianism and the technique of Virgil's own art. It is a romantic idyl of between five and six hundred lines in length, full of beauties of rhythm and felicities of language, but almost as full of weaknesses or absurdities. It is saturated throughout with Virgilian phrases; yet it is quite certainly an original poem, not a Virgilian cento like those which flooded the world at the time of the decay of Latin literature. For long it was an enigma; it is only some twenty years ago that one of the most brilliant and acute of modern German scholars, the late Professor Skutsch of Breslau, established it, by a study which is a model of analysis, as the work of Gallus in the early time when he and Virgil were studying and writing poetry in the closest intimacy, and in some sense therefore their joint work. In the Sixth and also in the Tenth *Eclogue,* Virgil has adroitly interwoven fragments of his friend's poetry. Likewise, whole lines and whole passages of the *Ciris,* besides almost countless phrases and turns of language, recur in the *Eclogues* and *Georgics* and even in the *Aeneid.* Whether, or where, or to what extent these in fact originated from Virgil's own hand it is impossible to determine. What Virgil lent, he had the right to resume. But what he borrowed — and he borrowed freely, as is well known, from his contemporaries no less than from his predecessors — he made his own by the mere act of deigning to take it. Such is the way of genius, and the prerogative, in poetry as in other arts, of supreme artists.

The other two pieces are of much maturer and more accomplished workmanship, but poetically of less interest. They belong to a somewhat later date, when the mechanism of the hexameter had been more fully mastered, and its structure and handling reduced to system. In both, the versification is undistinguishable from Virgil's; but the actual authorship remains, and is likely to remain, matter of inconclusive debate. The shorter but more masterly of the two, the *Moretum,* is a highly-finished idyl of farm-life. It is said to be closely copied from a Greek original, which however is not extant. On the internal evidence alone, were that supported by any adequate external testimony, it could be accepted without hesitation as Virgil's work; as a sort of cabinet-picture from his hand, one of the many exercises produced by him, while he was practising for the *Georgics,* which he did not leave a mere sketch but wrought out to elaborate completeness. But the only external testimony that we possess is the worthless ascription of this poem to Virgil, in a collection made in the sixth century.[12] That so fine a piece of work, known or believed to be by Virgil's own hand, should be left unmentioned by all his early biographers and commentators is almost incredible. It is just possible however that it had for long wholly disappeared and was not known to exist.

The third piece, the *Culex*, presents an equally perplexing problem. That Virgil wrote a poem so named is as certain as anything well can be. It is repeatedly mentioned by writers of the first century A.D., and mentioned as his without any doubt or qualification. Among those writers is the poet Statius, who in such a matter could hardly be mistaken; for he was both a poet and a scholar, and studied Virgil with nothing short of worship.[13] That this was not the poem which has come down to us, there is no reason at all for supposing. But it is not (or so we think) good enough to be Virgil's; it has no touch of the Virgilian magic.

There seem to be only two possible solutions of the puzzle. One is that we have here the work of some unknown contemporary, belonging to the same school or circle, who had caught Virgil's manner, and whose verbal and metrical technique can hardly be distinguished from his: the other is that the *Culex* is a carefully finished exercise by Virgil himself which, though he did not publish it or acknowledge it himself, somehow got into circulation. If we accept this latter theory, it will be one more instance of the general truth that the work even of the greatest artists — of Virgil, as of Phidias or Mozart or Raphael — has its mechanical side, and that it may sometimes be little more than skilful mechanism. To realize this does not make us value their genius less, but more. The work of genius grows more wonderful as we come to understand the labour that goes with it, the steady exercise of mere craftsmanship, the patient pursuit of a daily profession. It is only thus that we realize how laborious the artist's life is, and how much of his hand and brain is necessarily spent on the tasks of a common workman. After reading the *Culex* we can pass with higher and with more intelligent admiration to the miracle of the *Georgics.*

## VI. THE GEORGICS: LIFE AT PEACE

THE *Georgics* were, in the full sense, a labour of love. But their composition was undertaken at the instance of, and even, as Virgil's own words *haud mollia iussa*[14] seem to imply, under some pressure from, Maecenas and the Imperial government. Virgil's fastidiousness had to be overcome, his absorption in endless study to be urged into the work of creation. The call was made on him to make the new poetry at once into an expression and a motive force of national life.

For a century, as we have seen, the Roman world had been subjected to shattering disturbance, political, economical and social. Foreign and civil wars had been almost continuous. An immense increase of wealth from the conquest or annexation of new territory had been followed and outrun by wasteful administration and profligate expenditure. The resources of the provinces were mercilessly exploited. The flower of the Italian population had been drafted into the armies. Agriculture, the staple industry of Italy and the foundation of its solid prosperity, had fallen into a deplorable condition. Much land was derelict and had relapsed into thicket or morass. The class of yeoman farmers whose industry, piety, and domestic virtue had made Rome great, was dwindling away. Many of them had perished in war; many more had a worse fate. Unable to face the competition of cheap foreign food-stuffs, raised by slave-labour, that poured in from all parts of the Mediterranean, and affected by the universal restlessness which had come over the world, they drifted into towns and became an unemployed and discontented proletariat, a loose ballast which was a constant danger to the ship of state as it laboured through the waves of political revolution. The corn-land, orchards and vineyards which had made Italy like one great garden, and had maintained a hardy and healthy peasantry, gave place to immense stretches of uncultivated pasturage, run by absentee proprietors who took no concern for them, and only inhabited by migratory troops of herdsmen and shepherds who were slaves and half savages. Discontent, and the craving for city life with its idleness and excitement, spread through all classes.

To check this process, to reinstate agriculture, to anchor the nation afresh on the motherland, was one of the chief aims of the new government. The disbanded armies were settled all over Italy in agricultural colonies. Scientific farming was studied and taught. Small holdings were created and subsidized, and *petite culture* sedulously fostered. The extant treatise of Varro *De Re Rustica,* published about the time when Virgil set to work on the *Georgics,* was one among many books written then, primarily to give practical guidance in rural management, but also, as a matter of hardly less importance, to vindicate farming as the proper concern of the rich and educated class. This it did by making a moral as well as a material appeal. It recalled the immemorial national tradition; it emphasized the unceasing interest and unfailing pleasure, the virtue and happiness of rural life. According to the old Roman teaching, which still held good among the conservative elements of society, agriculture was the single form of "gain-getting" occupation which was worthy of a free Roman citizen, as it had in fact been the occupation of the heroic figures in Roman history. The times when the Consul was called to office from the plough, and returned to the plough from office, were over. But their spirit lingered in memory, and could be recalled. Something more was yet to be done for this. To give further impulse and sanction to the movement, in a time when education was widely spread and literature had become a force in public affairs, the aid of poetry was invoked. Men's eyes turned for this to Virgil as already the recognized head of living poets.

It was a task which, difficult as it might be, appealed to all his instincts, and one for which he was peculiarly qualified. His love of nature was deep and impassioned. He was familiar from childhood with farm work and rural life. Prolonged study and constant practice had made him a complete master, not only of his chosen vehicle, the Latin hexameter, but of the whole technique of the art of poetry. The plan of the *Georgics* opened before him as a thing which neither in Greek nor in Latin had yet been done: to produce a poem of rural life which should be at once largely national and fully human. In it he embodied portraiture born of intimate knowledge and loving observation, crowded with romantic association and literary ornament, heightened with motives of history and patriotism. Into it, with unequalled splendour of language, he infused his own deepest religious and philosophic thought, his brooding sense of an universal life, and that grave tenderness in which he stands even now alone.

To criticize the *Georgics* as though they were a technical treatise on husbandry, a handbook for farmers, is to miss their whole meaning. It is easy to point out that their descriptions and directions are (though extraordinarily accurate) neither systematic nor complete; that their wealth of allusion requires a highly trained reader to understand, much more to appreciate; that they pass beyond the literal scope of their theme to deal with nature and human life in their largest meaning. What they were designed to do, and what they did with triumphant beauty, was to embody in exquisite poetry an ideal, an imaginative vision, that of a life at peace with itself and in harmony with nature. They draw a living picture of a world of simplicity and industry, of hard work and true happiness. Virgil's "divine country" is not a fanciful Arcadian paradise.

Frost-bound winters and parching summers, storm and drought and flood, disease and blight, incessant toil and overshadowing death — *labor et durae inclementia mortis* — are all shewn in it. Yet the *divini gloria ruris* which is his theme is hardly distinguishable, in virtue of the natural magic with which he penetrates it, from the Golden Age of the Fourth *Eclogue.* It was a glory attainable and actual in the Italy which he loved so passionately.

"The praises of Italy," *laudes Italiae,* concentrated in the noble episode of the second book (ll. 136–176), are the central motive of the whole poem. They became applied to it as a sort of second title. From the Tyrolese mountain-pastures among their castellated rocks, right down to the Calabrian forests and the great stretches of corn-land in the Apulian plains, there is no part of Italy left untouched in the picture: lake and mountain, hill-fortress and river-valley, coast and bay. In the *Georgics,* the Italy of poets and painters took shape for the first time and once for all. The vignettes of foreign countries, of Greece, Egypt, Anatolia, of the Scythian steppe and the African desert, of half-unknown realms in the rich and fabulous East, are introduced with exquisite skill so as to reinforce by contrast this central picture of the lady of lands, the *donna e reina* of later Italian poets.

This was by itself a superb achievement. But it was not all. Virgil's interpretation and idealization of the Mother-country is interpenetrated with the ideals of a life lived in harmony with nature, of piety and simplicity, of unambitious happiness, of prosperous peace, of Roman virtue. And behind all these is his own profound humanity, his tenderness, his intense sympathy with all life, that of beasts and birds, of trees and flowers, even of winds and stars; and, deepest of all, his majestic sadness, his sense of the wonder and mystery of the world.

The seven years bestowed on a poem of little over two thousand lines (less than a line a day, as it has been put arithmetically) were well spent over work which was even more a labor of distillation and rejection than of composition. As it left his hands, Virgil was for once satisfied with his own work. But a few years later it was subjected to a strange vicissitude. The poem had originally ended with an episode devoted, as the conclusion of the *Eclogues* had been, to the praise of Gallus.

Since then, Gallus had climbed fast and far. He had been one of the generals at Actium, and there had been committed to him the vice-royalty of Egypt, a post which carried with it the keys of the Eastern Mediterranean world. The victory over Antony and the death of Cleopatra were, so far as indications or inferences enable us to judge, interwoven in this episode with a sketch of the historic wonders of Egypt. But Gallus, intoxicated by success, lost his head; he was recalled in disgrace; his fortune was confiscated, he was put on trial and sentenced to exile, and in the Roman manner, he fell on his own sword. The *Georgics* were recalled, and the conclusion cancelled and re-written. What we have lost by that disaster we cannot tell; some of the cancelled matter was pretty certainly used again by Virgil in the Eighth book of the *Aeneid,* and possibly elsewhere. What we have gained is the matchless episode of Orpheus and Eurydice. Its beauty silences criticism. But notwithstanding the great skill with which it is introduced, it could not be made, and it is not, an organic element in the structure of the poem. Yet we can hardly regret the enforced deviation from an otherwise rounded and faultless unity, when we consider that it not only gives us an unequalled masterpiece of feeling and expression, but adds to the *Georgics,* with an art beyond art, that last touch of haunting imperfection which makes Virgil more human, closer to ourselves, "not too steadfastly felicitous or too divinely alien to console." [15]

It was one result of the slow distillation of the *Georgics,* of the infinite pains taken by Virgil in refining and rejecting, that though there is nowhere an idle line or a wasted word, the poem never hurries. It is leisurely in its smooth movement; peace seems to rest upon it. Virgil had fully mastered the art, in Dryden's celebrated phrase, of "saying much in little, and often in silence." He can get more volume of melody, more wealth of harmonic suggestion, into a few words than any other poet. His descriptions of sky and weather, of soils and crops, of the instruments of husbandry and the life of the farm have, with close truth to nature, a stateliness like Milton's and a natural magic as intense as that of Keats. It is here and there in *Paradise Lost* —

> *So high above the circling canopy*
> *Of night's extended shade, from Eastern point*

*Of Libra to the fleecy star that bears*
*Andromeda far off Atlantic seas;*

or in *Hyperion* —

*The nightingale had ceased, and a few stars*
*Were lingering in the heavens, while the thrush*
*Began calm-throated. Throughout all the isle*
*There was no covert, no retired cave*
*Unhaunted by the murmurous noise of waves;*

that we come nearest to the Virgilian splendour and the Virgilian magic, as they glow for instance in passages like —

Solis ad occasum, cum frigidus aëra vesper
Temperat et saltus reficit iam roscida luna,
Litoraque alcyonem resonant, acalanthida dumi;[16]

or the incomparable —

Praeterea tam sunt Arcturi sidera nobis
Haedorumque dies servandi et lucidus Anguis,
Quam quibus in patriam ventosa per aequora vectis
Pontus et ostriferi fauces temptantur Abydi.[16]

Even single lines of technical statement,

Area cum primis ingenti aequanda cylindro —
Multa adeo gelida melius se nocte dedere —
Quin etiam caeli regionem in cortice signant —

even the terms of formal exposition taken over by him from the usage of Lucretius — *saepe etiam, nec tamen, praeterea, quod superest* — acquire in his handling poetical quality and unaccountable beauty.

Perhaps no poetry has ever been written which combines in such perfection richness of colour with purity of line, which is so exquisite in its transitions and so suave in its modulations, so smoothly gliding and nobly sustained. All these qualities are reinforced or culminate in the episodes, where the current of the poem spreads into large pools of beauty. Special attention may be called to some of these: in the First Book, the opening invocation to the Gods of the Country; the noble description of the world with its girdling zones and the march of the constellations through the heavens; the signs and wonders which overcame the earth with dreadful presage in the Civil War; in the Second Book, the matchless Praise of Italy, and the picture of the two ideal lives, the one of high philosophy reaching to heaven and treading fear and fate under foot, the other of simple and joyful community with nature, where God is also —

Fortunatus et ille, deos qui novit agrestis!

in the Third Book, the pageant imagined as celebrating not only the supremacy of Rome but the full conquest of poetry, with the Muses themselves brought from their Aonian height to the banks of the Mincio; and the description, with its strange haunting beauty, of the cattle-plague that desolated the lovely Tyrolese uplands and the Venetian plain; and in the Fourth Book, besides the idyl of Aristaeus into which the episode of Orpheus and Eurydice is woven, there is the lovely sketch of a fifth book on gardening — a picture within the picture — with its description of the "old man of Corycus," the ex-pirate who had settled down in perfect happiness as a florist and market-gardener under the walls of Tarentum. *Praetereo atque aliis post me memoranda relinquo;* with these words Virgil resumes his theme. But what he did not do still remains unaccomplished.

A deeper music still was to be drawn from him in the *Aeneid,* with a higher reach and a vaster sweep. But the golden cadence of poesy (in Shakespeare's phrase) was now found; and the *Georgics* remain as one of the few examples in art of attained perfection, no less than of that final imperfection which is at the soul of all art, as of all life. "The best poem of the best poet" Dryden incisively calls the *Georgics* in the dedicatory preface to his own translation; and here it may be said that no translation can convey their music, or give more than a faint image of the Virgilian colour and tone. A little later, Addison described them, in terms which if they sound frigid are at all events strictly true, as "the most complete, elaborate, and finished piece of all antiquity." Later praises have been expressions, in the language of their time, of the same feeling. Tennyson, more than any one else, has conveyed the note and charm of the *Georgics* in lines so familiar as hardly to require citation —

*Thou that singest wheat and woodland,*
*tilth and vineyard, hive and horse and herd;*
*All the charm of all the Muses*
*often flowering in a lonely word.*

They recapture, with wonderful felicity, the inimitable music of Virgil's own verse.

## VII. CONCENTRATION ON THE EPIC

IN THE prologue to the third book of the *Georgics,* Virgil mentions his purpose of approaching a still greater task, the celebration, in an historical epic, of the wars of Augustus Caesar and the annals of his line from the mythologic ancestry of Troy. The three lines in which he does so —

> Mox tamen ardentis accingar dicere pugnas
> Caesaris et nomen fama tot ferre per annos,
> Tithoni prima quot abest ab origine Caesar [17]

are structurally and rhythmically detachable, and give the impression of an added afterthought. Alone in the *Georgics,* they could be omitted without loss, or even, as we may incline to think, with advantage. They seem to shew the influence not only of his own projected purpose, but of something like response to external pressure put on him to pledge himself to its fulfilment.

" Kings and battles " had, as we have seen,

been Virgil's early ambition in poetry and the subject of his youthful exercises. Whether these were epic of the established type, dealing, in the Greek manner, with the heroic age,

> "*Presenting Thebes or Pelops' line*
> *Or the tale of Troy divine,*"

or handling the ancient semi-legendary Italian history, or whether they were built on recent and contemporary events, there is no clear evidence and no secure inference. All these kinds were being discussed and attempted by many poets: all, as we know from unmistakable allusions in his own earlier poems, were floating in Virgil's mind. So were various combinations of them. For the full achievement of Latin poetry, a Latin epic was called for; and to be Latin in the full sense, it must be national, or at least informed by the national spirit and temper.

Ennius had shewn the way; he had proved that such a thing was possible. His *Annals*, though they were less an epic than a chronicle, had established themselves as a Latin classic. They were on all men's lips, and were at once a schoolbook and a storehouse. It remained to carry what he had effected to a higher plane and give it a larger content; to produce a great Latin poem which should be a national epic in the largest sense, which might be for Rome and Italy, and for the Roman world through them, something like what Homer had been for Greece. This was, through all the intervening years, the goal which Virgil kept before him, the aim on which his mind slowly concentrated. The field open to him was vast: the leading motives were numerous, complex, and not easily reconcileable. Among them, no less than twelve may be specifically named:

1. The work must be a national poem in the full sense, embodying the pageant of Roman history, the portraiture of Roman virtue, the mission and the supremacy of Rome;

2. It must establish and vindicate the vital interconnection of Rome with Italy, and register the birth, which was only then taking effect, of a nation;

3. It must link up Rome and the new nation to the Greek civilization, as that had manifested itself in mythology and history, in art and letters, in the Hellenization which had spread into the Western portion of the Mediterranean world;

4. It must emphasize the Roman State and

the Italian people as not derivative from Greece, but of distinct and actually hostile origin, and absorbing or superseding Greek supremacy; and treat the conquest of the Greek world by Rome as the entrance on a predestined inheritance;

5. It must bring well into the foreground of the picture the historic conflict between Rome and Carthage, which was the greatest event in Roman history, which determined its subsequent course, and which fixed the limit to the sphere of the Asiatic races;

6. It must celebrate the feats of heroes, great deeds in battle and council and government, such as had lent immortal greatness to the *Iliad* and *Odyssey;*

7. It must find expression for the romantic spirit, in its two principal fields of love and adventure;

8. It must possess direct vital human interest, and create men and women drawn to the heroic scale and on the heroic plane, and yet embodying the qualities and passions and emotions of actual life;

9. It must connect its figures with larger and more august issues; with the laws of nature and the decrees of fate, the workings of a

mysterious Providence, and the sense of human destinies as at once moulding, and interpreted by, the human soul;

10. It must exalt the new régime, and give shape and colour to its ideals of peace and justice, development and reconstruction, ordered liberty, beneficent rule;

11. It must draw the lineaments of an ideal ruler, *pater patriae,* who should hold sovereignty as the chief servant of the commonwealth; and shew him as gravely conscious of his mission, rising towards its high demands, subordinating to it all thoughts of ease or luxury, all allurements of pleasure and temptations of the senses;

12. It must lift itself into a yet higher sphere, so as to touch the deepest springs of religion and philosophy, opening windows into the invisible world and kindling a pilot-light for the future.

Such were the motives, not indeed thus numbered and set forth as in a catalogue, but interfused with one another, which wrought in Virgil's mind; such was the complex web which he sought, so far as that were possible, to combine into organic unity in a single great poem. It is no wonder that the mere laying-out of the framework into which all these inter-related motives could be fitted was the task of years; and that, even when it had taken shape in its main outlines, the difficulties of its realization filled him with terror and brought him near to despair. *Tanta incohata res est,* are his own words in a letter to the Emperor of which a fragment has been preserved, *ut paene vitio mentis tantum opus ingressus mihi videar:*[18] "I think myself almost mad to have embarked upon it." To the last this feeling continued, heightening and heightened by the natural melancholy of his temperament; it took its final and most acute expression when, on his death-bed, he vainly begged that the *Aeneid* might be destroyed, and would have destroyed it with his own dying hands.

The magnetic field — to use a metaphor from science — within which the material for this poem gathered itself and took shape and structure, lay between and around two poles. These were, first, the historic climax of his own time in which the Roman Peace was established and the Roman Empire organized by Augustus; secondly, the legendary beginnings of Rome, and the mythical descent of the Roman people, and of the Julian family in particular, from the fugitive colonists of Troy. For this latter motive, the originating point of the whole imaginative fabric, he had a tradition to start from, which was already familiar. The story of a migration to Italy of the Trojan exiles under Aeneas grew up during the period of Greek colonization in the West. After Rome became a Mediterranean power, it was, in one version or another, very generally accepted; and with each generation new detail was added. It was popularized at Rome by Naevius in his chronicle-epic of the first Punic War. He, perhaps for the first time, and at the suggestion of a chronology adopted by some Greek historians which made the foundations of Rome and Carthage contemporaneous, interwove with it a visit of Aeneas to Carthage. Varro, the most learned of Roman antiquarians of the first century B.C., had, from many obscure sources, wrought this up into a detailed narrative. But the love of Dido and its tragic issue were, so far as the evidence enables us to judge, Virgil's own imaginative invention. It was one which originated a deathless legend and some of the noblest and most moving poetry in the world.[19]

For the remainder of the skeleton or structure of this epic, Virgil had not so much to invent as to select and harmonize from an enormous mass of fragmentary and often conflicting legend, both Greek and Latin. He had definitely rejected two plans: that on the one hand of a chronicle-poem on the lines followed by his Latin predecessors; that on the other hand which he had been urged to take both by court-pressure and by the prevalent tendency of fashion, of a poem the main scenes and action of which should be contemporary. But here his real difficulties only began. He had to create a world in which to place his action. He had to fix and observe the limits demanded in order to secure, within his chosen frame-work, epic unity and dramatic tension. He had to make his story credible, interesting, human. Yet he had so to construct it as to give scope for all the motives mentioned above. He had to preserve, through a fabric of unexampled complexity, a single large pattern, a single dominating tone. The artist must not be overwhelmed by the material, or lose breadth of handling in laborious refinement of workmanship.

Virgil then had to lay his foundations deliberately and carefully. There is no reason to question, on theoretic grounds, the statement of Donatus [20] that he drew out, in prose, a detailed sketch-plan of the contents of his *Aeneid*, divided into books, and that he kept this by him for reference and guidance in working on one or another part of the poem. This bears out what from internal evidence alone is sufficiently clear, that the composition of the *Aeneid* was not continuous. Portions which come later were composed before others which come earlier. The scheme underwent modifications, during the progress of composition, in important particulars. As published after his death it was not yet what he meant to make it. The editors performed their difficult task with great skill and judgment, but they could not do what Virgil himself had left undone. Of what they actually did they do not appear to have left any written record. But the general principle on which they proceeded is expressly stated: it was to cancel where necessary, but to add nothing—*hac lege ut superflua demerent, nihil adderent tamen.*[21] The *Aeneid* as they found and left it contains a certain number of inconsistencies, repetitions, and awkwardnesses of handling or transition. There were in it several gaps, and quite a considerable number of passages tentatively, perhaps marginally, inserted by Virgil's hand, and not yet decisively adopted nor fully incorporated. Some of these, we are told, were struck out by the editors, and four such have been actually preserved. It was clearly Virgil's object to keep the poem fluid, as far as possible, up to the last moment. The *Aeneid,* as we possess it, is the product of an immense mass of raw material, all of it worked upon, but still in process of undergoing large revision; yet in the main so nearly approaching to its final shape that it has been for the world at large a completed work of art. Careful study and minute analysis enable us to distinguish in it what may be called strata of composition, and to surmise, with greater or less probability, a good deal of Virgil's actual processes. We can assign the relative date of certain parts; we can trace the insertion or expansion, the re-casting or cancellation of certain episodes or passages. That enquiry is perilous to pursue too far, but is fascinatingly interesting. It can be pursued effectively only by highly trained investigators; and only by those among them whose scholarship is combined with delicate artistic sense and with some faculty of imaginative divination.

One instance may be cited as illustrative, because it is on a large scale and involves comparatively simple problems. The third book of the *Aeneid* differs in style, and is at a different stage of structure, from all the others. It gives the story of Aeneas' adventures, from the departure from Troy up to the arrival in Sicily, as related by him to Dido at Carthage, in continuation of his narrative of the fall of Troy. Its construction is clear evidence not only of its unfinished state, but of its early composition. It contains passages, particularly at the beginning and end, in the dry, annalistic manner of Virgil's predecessors, which we may say with confidence are youthful work, anterior to the *Georgics*. Inserted in it are lumps of rather laboured material, easily detachable from their context (e.g., ll. 414–428, 445–452, 575–582). The substance, and even the wording, of the episode of Achaemenides (ll. 588–654) has been largely drawn upon, and used to better effect, for the episode of Laocoön in the second book; and it is not impossible that Virgil would have struck it out entirely. Throughout, except in the opening and concluding lines, and in the beautifully managed episode of the meeting with Helenus and Andromache, the narrative is curiously impersonal, as though told by a chronicler, and in sharp contrast to Book II, which is saturated from beginning to end with the personality and emotion of the narrator. In ten or a dozen places at least there are lines or phrases quite unsuitably put in the mouth of Aeneas, scraps of history or archaeology, and even references to the subsequent history of places mentioned. There are also marked, if minor, discrepancies from the rest of the poem, as when Helenus prophesies to Aeneas that the Sibyl will tell him what in fact is told him by the glorified spirit of Anchises.

Recent research, with the more delicate analysis possible to modern scholarship, has found the clue. It has established beyond reasonable doubt that the substance of this book was originally written as direct narrative, and was in fact the first book of the poem. Two-thirds of it at least can be reinstated in that form with slight verbal changes, most of which can be made even without disturbing the metre. The clue, once grasped, enables us not only to explain what had always been perplexing difficulties, but to get, as it were, inside Virgil's workshop and follow the processes of his workmanship. The alteration of plan, with its consequent changes so far as these were actually carried out, was almost certainly made within four years of Virgil's death, and the final remodelling of Book III was never effected. It is both interesting and illuminating to think it away, and to see how Dido's request with which Book I closes — with the omission of the last two lines, which are an obvious connecting link added when the change was made — is fulfilled in Book II, and with what swiftness of beauty Book IV then follows on at once. Yet there were good reasons for the change. It would have been a grave defect in art to open the poem with a mass of purely introductory matter, and one still graver not to set the stage at once for the main action. It would also, it may be judged, have been a mistake to place the high-tension work of the second and fourth books together without some intermediate relief. But nowhere else in the *Aeneid* do we miss so much the absence of the artist's final hand.

Virgil's concentration on the *Aeneid* knew no limit. In the extant fragment of his letter to Augustus, already cited, he goes on to speak of this in very striking words, said very simply: "besides, as you know, I am bestowing other and far higher studies on it as well" — *alia quoque studia multoque potiora.* He was going deep into national traditions. He was mastering many volumes not only of Greek and of earlier Latin poetry, but of history, archaeology, science. He was making a profound study of Italian religion and Greek speculation. He was travelling much in Central and Southern Italy to study its natural features, to collect local legends, to familiarize himself with racial and tribal characteristics or usages. As he grew older, the pursuit of philosophy, the meaning of the world and the faith or doctrine of a future life, became his more and more absorbing study. Into the *Aeneid* meanwhile he kept pouring accumulated learning and profound thought. Already a national epic, it insensibly transformed itself into something still greater, an epic of civilization and humanity. He became not only the voice of Rome, *Romanus Vergilius,* but the poet and prophet of mankind.

## VIII. THE STRUCTURE OF THE AENEID

THE structure of the *Aeneid* as it finally shaped itself may at this point be briefly set out. To grasp it as a whole is necessary towards any adequate appreciation of its movement, of the manipulation by Virgil of its complex motives, and of the large unity which he sought to give, and succeeded marvellously in giving, to matter which as we have seen was not only of great range but of unusual intricacy.

Structure, in all the arts, bears an organic relation to scale. The length of an epic poem was already, within wide limits, indicated by usage and precedent. The *Iliad* and *Odyssey* had set a model. They had shown a limit which allowed full amplitude of treatment, and which it was desirable not to exceed; within which, the epic handling had free scope, and beyond which, the risk arose of losing effective unity and causing fatigue through excess of detail or dissipation of interest. Even with such an unequalled masterpiece as the *Iliad,* the fifteen thousand lines to which it had grown by successive expansions and insertions involved real difficulty in securing cohesion. The lesser size of the *Odyssey* — twelve thousand lines, with the ending which was recognized by the best Greek critics as an epilogue or accretion, not much more than eleven thousand without it — was tacitly accepted as a working maximum. We may reasonably suppose that a compass of about ten thousand lines was in Virgil's mind when he began to lay out the plan of the *Aeneid.* As we possess it, it has 9,896; and there is no reason to think that further revision would have very materially altered that figure.

It is interesting to observe that, partly from the influence of Virgil's example, partly from practical experience, this is the scale which has on the whole been followed by later poets. In the instances to be cited, the figures are given in round numbers. Lucan's unfinished *Pharsalia* has 8,000 lines; Statius' *Thebaid* is very nearly of the same length as the *Aeneid.* After the decay of letters, a long gap follows. The *Chanson de Roland,* an epic lay rather than an epic in the full sense, is of 4,000 lines only. Boccaccio's *Teseide,* the first achievement in epic of the earlier Renaissance, is by design or coincidence of exactly the same length to a line as the *Aeneid.* The medieval romances set themselves no such limit, nor did the romantic epics of the later Renaissance: the *Roman de la Rose* has nearly 23,000 lines, the *Orlando Innamorato* over 35,000, the *Orlando Furioso* 40,000. Tasso's *Gierusalemme Liberata,* written when that tide of exorbitance had not quite exhausted itself, runs to 15,000. But the *Paradise Lost* with its 10,500 lines resumed the classical tradition; and to come down at once to modern times, *Sigurd the Volsung,* the greatest if not indeed the only English epic of the Victorian Age, is of about the same length. The literary epics of the Alexandrian School had taken shorter flights on a feebler wing. The *Argonautica* of Apollonius, which Virgil studied minutely and used largely, sinks exhausted and comes to a dead stop when still a good way short of 6,000 lines.

The *Iliad* and *Odyssey* had, centuries before Virgil's time, been divided for facility of reference, as also for purposes of recitation, into twenty-four books each. But that division was quite arbitrary. It was determined simply by the obvious convenience of naming the sections by the twenty-four letters of the full Greek alphabet. Virgil, for reasons which we may imagine but need not insist upon, chose to arrange his own epic in twelve books; and the draft-sketch on which he worked seems from the first to have been so subdivided. The action of the poem extends from the fall of Troy down to the final pacification in Italy. But its earlier portion, by a device adapted from the *Odyssey,* is set as a picture within the picture, in the form of a narrative recounted by the hero at the Carthaginian Court. By the use of this device, Virgil is enabled to open his poem, not with what must necessarily have been either a mere summary recapitulation or a somewhat languid and dilatory narration, but with the highly dramatic episode of the storm at sea and the arrival at Dido's newly founded capital. This is the subject of Book I. It sets the scene and introduces the central figure at once; it excites immediate interest by a rapid succession of vivid and picturesque incidents; and through the intervention of the gods from point to point, it gives scope for setting forth, in clear outline, the great issues involved and the purposes of destiny.

Having thus set his scene and got his action into full movement, Virgil proceeds to deploy his epic. Book I ends with the description of the banquet in the Carthaginian palace. The whole of Book II is occupied with the story of the "last agony of Troy." It is told by Aeneas, in a narrative of unsurpassed splendour, and with all the dramatic force which comes of its being filled with the narrator's personality. *Quaeque ipse miserrima vidi et quorum pars magna fui,* Aeneas' opening words, are the key-note of the whole narrative.

The same is formally true of Book III, in which Aeneas continues the story of his adventures from the fall of Troy up to his landing on the Carthaginian Coast. But as has been explained in the last chapter, this book was only partially remodelled in its present form, and was left by Virgil at his death in a very imperfect state. The change from chronicle to personal narrative was not easy to make. We cannot put any limit to the skill and success with which Virgil might have carried it out to completion; we may safely assume that he would have altered those passages in which Aeneas speaks as though he had forgotten both the occasion and the audience, and that he would have wrought the whole book more into tone, though it would have remained, and rightly so for the purposes of dramatic relief, poetry of a lower temperature than either of the two magnificent episodes which precede and follow it. For in the story of the fall of Troy he had put forth the height of his power; and the story of the love of Dido and its tragic issue had, beyond his first intention and almost against his will, taken hold of him, expanded to a greatness and deepened into an intensity unsurpassed in ancient or modern poetry.

This episode fills the whole of Book IV. It has, in all ages, been the part of the *Aeneid* which has outshone, has even in some sense eclipsed the rest, by its fusion of delicate psychological insight with human sympathy, of splendid eloquence with burning passion. The famous outburst in St. Augustine's *Confessions*,[22] with its cry of hysterical renunciation — *Deus vita mea, quid miserius flente Didonis mortem quae fiebat amando Aeneam, non flente autem mortem meam quae fiebat non amando te!* — is but a single expression of the power with which Virgil's Dido has held the world entranced. It might be, and has been, claimed that in this book Virgil reaches his highest achievement. Yet if we were to accept this view, it might be difficult to deny the consequential judgment that, while accomplishing a miracle, he had made the *Aeneid* reach its climax of human interest too early, and on what from the larger structural point of view is, however splendid in itself, an episode, a secondary issue.

It is with some such feeling, at all events, that we pass from Book IV to Book V, with its quiet unfolding of the story from the putting to sea from Carthage to the resumption of the voyage to Italy in its final stage. The scene here lies in Sicily; and more than half the book is occupied with the elaborate description of the funeral games held there on the anniversary of the death of Anchises. That whole episode is so handled as to have a tranquillizing and reinforcing effect on the progress of the main action, in which it is an interlude. The band of exiles have now been disciplined into a little commonwealth, prepared to strike root in their destined home, and conscious that the long wanderings are now nearing an end. A change has insensibly come over Aeneas himself. He has passed through a new experience. He is older and wiser, more fully aware of his responsibility and his mission, though he still has to seek and to find more enlightenment. It is a new generation, one might almost say a redeemed people, whom he now leads forth. His son Ascanius has shot up in a year from childhood to gallant boyhood. The older and feebler of his following are left behind to settle down among Sicilian friends and kinsfolk. Juno's attempt to burn the ships is foiled. The fleet sets sail with smooth seas and favorable breezes. *Datur hora quieti.* The incident with which the book ends, the loss of Palinurus in mid-passage, with its strange dreamy beauty, only seems to complete the sense of charmed peace, the lull between the many tasks accomplished and the rising of the curtain on the final task now to be met and fulfilled.

Here the transition takes place. Hitherto all has been prelude and preparation, enlarged and enriched by the Trojan, Carthaginian and Sicilian episodes. But before opening his main scene, Virgil interposes what is not so much an episode as an intermezzo. He ascends into a higher sphere. In Book VI the action is superhumanized, and passes, as it were, beyond the boundaries of space and time. Landing at Cumae, Aeneas passes, under the guidance of the Sibyl and with the Golden Bough for his passport, into the other world. He descends into a mysterious realm under earth; he sees unrolled before him the past and the future. He is shewn the world of the dead, and the world of those who are not yet alive. He crosses the River of Forgetfulness; he traverses the Mourning Fields; he is shewn the Judgment appointed after death, and given a glimpse into Hell and its punishments. Then he lays down the Golden Bough and moves on into Elysium, where the spirit of his father receives him, expounds to him the cycle of destiny and the doctrine of immortality, and passes before him the long pageant of his own descendants, the heroic and historic figures of the Roman race, with a culminating vision of the establishment of the universal empire. When he reascends to earth through the Gate of Sleep, it is as one initiated, consecrated, lifted into a higher atmosphere and given the assured promise of deity. He is now no longer the groping follower, but the conscious and elect instrument, of the Providence that moves the worlds.

Having reached this point, we are now in a

position to grasp the architecture of the whole poem, as it reveals itself from an elevated central point of view. What is to come is the main subject of the epic: the conquest and settlement, the conclusion, after a short but eventful war, of peace and alliance, and the laying of the foundations, with full concord among the confederated peoples and the reconciled deities, for the realm of the "lords of the world," *rerum dominos,* the Italian nation and the Roman State. What has preceded is now seen to be a magnificent prelude converging on this issue. It might be put in the terms of an art cognate to that of poetry. One may compare the structure which Virgil planned and executed to a basilica, approached through a triple-bayed narthex (Books I, III, V), with two splendid and elaborately adorned flanking halls (Books II and IV), and a great central dome (Book VI). These among them fill an equivalent space to the basilica itself, and are wrought with it into a single architectural composition.

At the opening of Book VII Virgil emphasizes the transition. This he does by a fresh invocation of the Muse; by the significant words *maior rerum mihi nascitur ordo,* which recall with an added depth of meaning the *magnus ab integro saeclorum nascitur ordo* of the Fourth *Eclogue;* and by a new prologue, making it clear that the scene of action is now Italy and the interest Italian. Having thus raised the curtain, he proceeds: *maius opus moveo,* "to the greater work I set my hand." He narrates the landing of the Trojan colonists at the Tiber mouth, the negotiations with King Latinus, the malignant intervention of Juno and the outbreak of hostilities, and ends with the great pageant of "the gathering of the clans," as Warde Fowler aptly called it, the muster-roll of the national Italian armies.

The stage is now fully set for the succeeding scenes, and the action unrolls itself steadily. Book VIII is mainly occupied with the embassy to Evander at the little rustic settlement which was to be the site of Rome, the alliance formed with him and with the Etruscans, and the preparations for the war which is now inevitable. Book IX contains the attack on the Trojan camp at Ostia by the confederate Italian armies under Turnus, and the famous episode of Nisus and Euryalus. In Book X Aeneas, arriving with the Etruscan fleet, reaches and relieves the beleaguered camp. A fierce battle ensues. It ends at nightfall in a complete Trojan victory, clouded by the death of young Pallas at the hand of Turnus. Book XI is one of rapid and crowded incident; the truce and the funeral rites over the slain, the council of the allied princes, the advance of Aeneas on the Latin capital, the renewed battle, and the beautifully told episode of the virgin-warrior Camilla. The scale dips heavily; the decisive end is felt approaching. It comes in Book XII, perhaps Virgil's greatest achievement of dramatic value, masterly construction, and faultless diction, for which he has reserved and now lets go his whole power. Terms of peace are solemnly made, to turn on the issue of a single combat between Aeneas and Turnus. They are broken, in a revulsion of Latin feeling under the influence of the still unappeased Juno. The madness of battle kindles anew, but "neither gods nor forces are equal." Aeneas is preparing to storm the Latin city, when Turnus, his eyes at last opened and his infatuation fallen away from him, calls a halt and faces his antagonist. In this pause and crisis, the reconciliation of the gods is at last effected. Destiny has its way. Turnus falls; and as his "indignant spirit flits into the dark," the expiation is accomplished and the new world may begin.

This summary sketch omits many constructional elements in the closely wrought fabric of the *Aeneid;* nor can it bring out, what would require a much fuller and more intimate study, the art with which the motives of the poem are linked up and intertwined with one another, and the guiding thread which runs through the whole, the gradual evolution and revelation of the divine purpose. But it may suffice to indicate the great skill of its construction and the unity of its design. For the plan of the *Aeneid,* once grasped in its main outline, will at least correct the superficial view (respectable in its antiquity but deplorable in its lack of appreciation) that Virgil attempted to combine in an overloaded structure the content of a Latin *Iliad* and a Latin *Odyssey,* and that the *Aeneid* falls apart into two halves, the first, like the *Odyssey,* a romance of adventure, the second, like the *Iliad,* an epic of war. This view remained current until quite recent times. "Virgil set himself," a fine scholar wrote in 1879, "to model his epic on the type of the *Iliad* and *Odyssey.* The first six books . . . were to be his *Odyssey;* the second six . . . were to be his *Iliad.*" [23] It was only a step from this to describe the whole thing as "a bastard mixture." We shall hardly even begin to appreciate the *Aeneid* until we realize that with all its complexity of structure and movement, with all its debt to both *Iliad* and *Odyssey,* it is no less than these an organic unity and a masterpiece of original creative art.

## IX. THE HUMAN ELEMENT

AMONG the qualities which give an epic poem permanent fame and enduring life, two are of the first importance: a great ideal which it embodies as an interpretation of history and of the world in which man finds himself; and a pervading human sympathy to which the human mind and heart, from one age to another, instinctively respond. In both these qualities the *Aeneid* is eminent. But it is probably through the latter that it has to most of its myriad readers made its first and also its last appeal. Virgil is the representative poet of the Imperial idea and of the Latin civilization on which both the Middle Ages and the modern world are based and built. But he is no less, he is even more, the poet in whom mankind have found the most perfect expression of their longings, their questionings, their aspirations; "giving utterance," in Newman's beautiful words, "as the voice of Nature herself, to that pain and weariness yet hope of better things which is the experience of her children in every time." [24]

In Homer, this deep human sympathy is present as an inner life, but only, so to say, in the germ. In Greek poetry of the central and classical period — the poetry which was concentrated in its utmost brilliance at Athens — it was kept under severe control; it was subordinated to an incomparably luminous, but, as those who have since re-sought the springs of Helicon have often been inclined to think, a somewhat hard intelligence. Roman sensibility was largely the creation of the later Greek or Alexandrian age. In the most popular poets of that school, that sensibility tended to get out of control. In their Latin pupils and successors, both before and after Virgil, this tendency was further exaggerated. Reaction from the austere Roman tradition, and the captivating charm of sentimental indulgence for the pleasure-loving Italian temperament, led to a sort of deliquescence. The Latin *mollities*, the Italian *morbidezza*, a delicacy passing into pulpy softness, is the word used to describe it. Fibre was weakened; sentiment became sentimentality. It was Virgil's aim, and it is perhaps his greatest achievement, to fuse the new romantic sensibility with the epic largeness and the Roman dignity.

To make a human being of the principal figure on his canvas was by no means an easy matter. Aeneas, by the fundamental scheme of the poem, had to be an idealized and symbolic character. He had to carry, *attollens umero famamque et fata nepotum,* the destinies of a race and a nation. He had to be a warrior and legislator, whose own life was subordinated throughout to the claims of public duty. He was weighted with the responsibilities of a founder, a restorer, a governor. The Achilles of the *Iliad* is a prince in the flush and ardour and selfishness of youth, full of the pride of life and only shadowed by foreknowledge of an early death. The Ulysses of the *Odyssey* is a man of wide experience and incomparable adroitness, who passes triumphantly through a series of exciting adventures on his return from Troy. He is fighting throughout for his own hand, for re-conquest of his home and re-union with his wife and child. Neither of them has any call to be a saint; Achilles has no regard for mercy, nor Ulysses for truth: but in neither figure is there any obstacle to the development of the purely individual human interest. With Aeneas it is different. He has done with the romance and gladness of youth. He is loaded with responsibilities not his own. He has no home to return to, no personal happiness to look forward to. He has to make a new home in a strange land, not for himself, but for his followers and his son. He has a loyal staff, but no intimate friend, no one with whom he can share his soul. He hates bloodshed and has no joy in battle, yet he has to wage a sanguinary war. His entanglement at Carthage brings him no pleasure while it lasts, and he breaks it off with a sombre acquiescence. His marriage at the close to the heiress of the Latin kingdom is a wholly political or dynastic arrangement, and for him, as for her, only one more sacrifice to duty. Of his last years Virgil is all but silent; he only lets us know that they were decreed to be few, and that he was thereafter to join the ranks of the gods — *siqua est ea gloria* — and in another world find the reward, such as it might be, of his lifelong labour of self-suppression.

A pathetic and a heroic figure, Virgil's Aeneas is nevertheless a little removed from humanity both in his virtues and in his shortcomings. If Aeneas be, as to some extent he is, an idealized Augustus, Marcus Aurelius, two hundred years later, is a re-embodied Aeneas. *Non sponte sequor,* the words wrung out of Aeneas on one of the few occasions when he nearly gives way to simple human emotion, might serve as the motto both for him and for Marcus. In both, they pass more and more from an accent of complaint into what is at once a confession of faith and a religious aspiration, nearly corresponding to *Thy will be done.*

*Pietas,* conscientiousness, the steady fulfilment of duty to God and man, is the central quality of Virgil's hero. The spring of his conduct from the first, it grows in power as the action proceeds. In the vision or initiation of his passage through the Underworld, he goes through, it has been suggestively said, a process something like that of conversion.[25] Thenceforth he has no thought of self, and is immune to temptations of the senses; he lives for his people and his mission. He is a pattern of patience and self-sacrifice, of courtesy and sympathy. A formidable warrior, he does all he can to avoid the issue of bloodshed, and to stop it when begun. In many great sayings, like the noble

> Pacem me exanimis et Martis sorte peremptis
> Oratis? equidem et vivis concedere vellem, [26]

he pleads for peace and reconciliation. Only at the death of Pallas, the boy who had been committed to his own special charge, do mingled grief and rage overcome his self-control and kindle into battle-fury. Of his shocking order for bound prisoners of war to be sent for immolation over Pallas' funeral pyre, one can only say that it is Virgil's single lapse into barbarism, and think or hope that the two lines might have been cancelled in his final revision. It shews the dark side of the Roman character. The horrible story of the *Arae Perusinae* after the capitulation of Perusia in the civil war of 41 B.C., — if it be true, which is perhaps doubtful; but it was believed — and the execution in cold blood after years of imprisonment of the heroic and chivalrous Vercingetorix, were events of contemporary history. We ourselves have in recent years seen atrocities as great perpetrated in the daylight by men who called themselves civilized and Christian. So thin is the crust which, now as then, separates mankind from the abyss.

It is not, however, in stray relics of savagery that the humanity of Virgil's hero is felt to fail. It is in his conduct to Dido. Many critics have conjectured that in the original scheme Dido was a Cleopatra or Alcina, a temptress from whose clutches Aeneas was to be rescued. If so, art proved greater than the artist; and his human sympathy, his insight into a woman's heart and a queen's passion, swept him away irresistibly. Apology may be invented; palliations may be urged: defence of Aeneas is impossible. "Upon the whole matter, and humanly speaking, I doubt there was a fault somewhere." Such is the beautifully felt and beautifully worded summing-up of Dryden. It is as wise as kind in its reticence; and we may leave it at that, for we cannot really go beyond it, and shall hardly improve upon it.

Dido is perhaps Virgil's greatest creation, and certainly one of the greatest in all poetry. She is suggested by and partly modelled on the Medea of Apollonius; but under Virgil's subtle and masterly hand she expands into something much greater. While she is there, she fills the whole canvas, and beside her, Aeneas fades and chills. Into her Virgil pours all his insight into the human heart and his sense of purely human tragedy. He gives her immortal life.

In the rest of the *Aeneid,* feminine interest is subordinate, unless the superhuman figures of Juno and Venus, so ably modelled and so skilfully contrasted, may be thought of as not merely goddesses but women. Creusa, the adored and adoring wife whom Aeneas lost in the sack of Troy, is but a graceful and lovely phantom. Lavinia, the young princess who carries the Italian kingdom as her dowry, is slightly drawn and kept deliberately in the background; she and her lover Turnus are not allowed to meet. Only in the episode of Camilla does Virgil bring another female figure into the front plane of the action. She is unique and alone:

Illam omnis tectis agrisque effusa iuventus
Turbaque miratur matrum et prospectat euntem, [27]

and Virgil lavishes his art on the portrait of the terrible maiden, *bellatrix* (" soldieress " is the fine Shakespearian word), who from infancy has lived " among the lonely hills " — *pastorum solis exegit montibus aevum,* — with rivers and forests for her companions, in a fierce and flawless virginity. His treatment here allows him to give full scope to romance, and to bring the essence of pastoral beauty into the august field of the epic. More even than the witchery of the *Eclogues,* this scene makes Virgil the fountain head of romanticism.

Not that his other women are negligible. Andromache in Epirus, Anna at Carthage, Silvia in the Latin woodland, are all touched by him into life. In the larger portrait of Queen Amata, in the tenderly modelled figure of the mother of Euryalus, and, at the very end, in the sisterly devotion of Juturna, his breadth of sympathy and fineness of touch are remarkable. But he lavishes that sympathy most on the portraiture of boys: on Ascanius, whom he follows lovingly through his growth, from the child who escaped from Troy clinging to his father's hand, to the princely figure in the flush of youth, *integer aevi,* who begins to take his place in council and battle; on Euryalus, Lausus, Pallas, flower-like forms over whom hangs the shadow of early death.

But it is not merely in this figure or that, it is throughout, that the Aeneid is saturated with human tenderness. A half-accidental isolation of two words from one of his great lines has given to the world, as the very essence of

Virgil's magic, as the keynote of the music which he draws out of life, the expression of "the tears of things," *lacrimae rerum.* In those half-lines of his, of which Newman wrote with a delicacy of appreciation that is like Virgil's own, this is the accent which recurs constantly. It is "the voice of Nature herself," but a human voice which reaches above and beyond Nature. It is present like a haunting music, playing round and interpreting the transitoriness, the brief sweetness of life — *breve et inreparabile tempus; veluti cum flos succisus aratro;* the shadowiness of fame — *si qua est ea gloria; longa oblivia potant;* the weight of gigantic superhuman forces — *stat sua cuique dies; dis aliter visum; ineluctabile fatum;* the longing for rest — *nos alias hinc ad lacrimas; vobis parta quies; felix morte tua neque in hunc servata dolorem;* the sorrow of departing and the keener grief over the departed — *dulces moriens reminiscitur Argos; fleti ad superos belloque caduci; salve aeternum mihi aeternumque vale;* the greatness of the human soul — *sancta ad vos anima descendam; vixi et quem dederat cursum Fortuna peregi, et nunc magna mei sub terras ibit imago;* the flickering light of an inextinguishable hope — *ripae ulterioris amore; aut videt aut vidisse putat; coniunx ubi pristinus illi respondet curis aequatque Sychaeus amorem.* In no other poetry are the chords of human sympathy so delicately touched, its tones so subtly interfused. In none is there so deep a sense of the beauty and sorrow of life, of keen remembrance and shadowy hope, and, enfolding all, of infinite pity.

## X. THE ITALO-ROMAN IDEAL

VIRGIL owed his immediate acceptance as the prince of Latin poets, and still owes his place among the supreme poets of the world, not merely to his insight into the life of man and nature, his majesty and tenderness, and the melodious perfection of his verse. Over and above all these, he was the interpreter, we may even call him the creator, of a great national ideal. That ideal was at once political, social and religious. The supremacy of Rome took in his hands the aspect of an ordinance of Providence, towards which all previous history had been leading up under divine guidance. It meant the establishment of an empire to which no limit of time or space was set, and in which the human race should find ordered peace, settled government, material prosperity, the reign of law and the commonwealth of freedom. *His ego nec metas rerum nec tempora pono,* such is the decree of the Lord of Heaven. The mission of "the Roman," of the Roman race envisaged as a single undying personality, is not only *regere imperio populos,* but *paci imponere morem,* to establish peace as the habit and usage of the world. This is to be effected by fusion of Roman strength with Italian piety, by the incorporation or consubstantiation of Rome with Italy.

The canonization of Rome, as a sort of living being, *Roma mater,* was effected, just at the same time, by the genius of Livy. Beyond that, Livy does not go; and his History has been called a funeral oration delivered, by the most loving and most eloquent of her children, over the grave of the Republic. Virgil's view reached still further, his aim was still higher. Rome was to reincarnate herself, and the Italo-Roman ideal, realized and established, was to be the light and life of the world.

To bring out this all-important point more clearly, some recapitulation is desirable, and we must extend our view over Virgil's whole work from beginning to end. As we have seen, Virgil was born midway in the process of fusion. A few years earlier, there had been a general Italian revolt against Rome. An Italian government, the first in history, had been set up, with the rival capital of Italica. It was an attempt, such as has been repeatedly and always disastrously made since, to create a unified Italy from which Rome should be excluded. During the time of Virgil's youth, the whole of Italy had been included in the Roman citizenship. But the spiritual union was harder to effect. Neither then, nor through nearly two thousand years thereafter, has it wholly been compassed.

Faintly and uncertainly in the *Eclogues,* clearly and fully in the *Georgics,* Virgil has this ideal of an Italian Rome and a Roman Italy before him. Latin was already the universal Italian speech. In the *Georgics,* the triumphant Roman language, wrought into a new splendour and sweetness, is consecrated to the Praises of Italy. Of set purpose, Virgil uses the terms *Italus* and *Romanus* interchangeably. The keynote of the *Georgics,* repeated and re-emphasized in the *Aeneid,* is their coalescence. The elect survivor of fallen Troy is sent forth to found a new city and nation in the West. His seven years of wandering are a pilgrimage, a crusade, through which the goal is slowly approached, and in the course of which his mission is gradually revealed to him by prophecies and portents, by divine communications, and finally by his initiation into the realms of the underworld, and the vision of the future there passed before him. In the final scene of the Reconciliation of the Gods, the crown is placed on the structure by a single majestic line linking the two names,

> Sit Romana potens Itala virtute propago.[28]

It is at once a prayer, a decree, and a benediction.

In this fusion of the *Itala virtus* with the *Romana potentia* [29] lay in Virgil's time — as it does, under altered names, in ours — the hope of the world. It was racked in every joint. Alongside of gigantic territorial expansion had gone rapid disintegration of the machinery of government. The Asiatic provinces had been drained and plundered. Spain and Gaul, in which the strength of the West lay, were disorganized, only half assimilated, seething with revolt. Agriculture in Italy had almost gone to ruin. Reckless commercial speculation had brought about something like a general collapse. The enormous wastage of the Civil Wars had left the treasury empty and the State bankrupt. Roman piety, Roman patriotism, seemed crumbling away. For the reconstruction of the new world there was needed a great effort of intelligence, a great re-establishment of production, and, above all, a great moral impulse. The task of Augustus when he returned from the East in 29 B.C. was something like that of Aeneas when he founded a new nation out of the wreckage of the Trojan War. The *Georgics* first, the *Aeneid* later and more fully, gave this task an imaginative embodiment. They recalled, with all the charm of poetry, the new generation into the old paths; and pointed them towards a new path in which the virtues of the past should be regained, in which a Roman Italy and an Italian Rome should go forward to rule and restore the world, should heal its wounds, give it peace and prosperity, bind it into one.

In the *Pollio,* the so-called Messianic Eclogue, we see this ideal forming, as something dimly descried and mystically imagined. A Golden Age, long foretold and now close on the horizon, is based on the doctrine, which for Virgil had a deep fascination, of the Great Year, a cycle of thousands of years which returned into itself and after completion recommenced its course. In the *Georgics* this prophetic vision is no longer seen in an iridescent haze; it has taken definite shape and clear outline. The Golden Age is a reality: the Golden World has come. It is his own Italy, here and now, such as it is, if the Italian people would but realize it, *sua si bona norint*. Not once in a cycle of many thousand years, but perpetually in the common revolution of the seasons, a golden age returns. The earth, that never grudges to its children or cheats its lovers, *iustissima tellus,* is the same through the generations; richly blessed, *fortunati nimium,* are those who live, as they may if they will, the old Italian life —

Hanc olim veteres vitam coluere Sabini —[30]

which is also the life by which Rome *rerum facta est pulcherrima,* became the crown-jewel of the world. In this passion of patriotism Virgil even idealizes Roman Italy into an earthly paradise; he creates the lovely and imperishable illusion of life lived in it as a pure delight. *Fundit humo facilem victum,* he says of this land of his; the golden peace of an Indian summer, *secura quies,* broods over it. The countryman has only to reach out his hand and take what Earth offers —

Quos rami fructus, quos ipsa volentia rura
Sponte tulere sua, carpsit; [31]

and in lines as melodious as any that ever came even from his pen, Virgil paints, and almost persuades us to believe, the labour of husbandry as merely the effort to keep up with the prodigal beneficence of Nature:

Nec requies, quin aut pomis exuberet annus
Aut fetu pecorum aut Cerealis mergite culmi
Proventuque oneret sulcos atque horrea vincat;
Venit hiems, teritur Sicyonia baca trapetis,
Glande sues laeti redeunt, dant arbuta silvae;
Et varios ponit fetus autumnus, et alte
Mitis in apricis coquitur vindemia saxis.[32]

But this lovely world of the *Georgics* is not even so the dream-world of the fourth *Eclogue*. Its magical beauty is relieved against a dark shadow. Over and over again Virgil comes back to the bitter truth of care, poverty, sickness, hard living — *patiens operum exiguoque adsueta iuventus;* of the doom of unceasing toil —

Pater ipse colendi
Haud facilem esse viam voluit; [33]

of parching summers and cruel winters, storm and flood, droughts and pestilences; of degeneration as the law not only for man but for Nature herself —

> Sic omnia fatis
> In peius ruere ac retro sublapsa referri; [34]

of the *angusti terminus aevi,* and the handful of dust in which all ends; and he begins to look wistfully to the faith or hope — *quidam dixere,* " some have named it " — of a life beyond this world.

In the *Aeneid,* these lines of thought and feeling converge towards a higher synthesis. *Gesta Populi Romani,* " the achievements of the Roman People," a title under which the *Aeneid* went even in Virgil's own lifetime, gives the import of the whole poem as the expression of the Italo-Roman ideal. The splendours of past history, the majesty of the actual Empire, the limitless future prophesied and decreed for the *Itala tellus* and the *Romana propago,* combine in his picture.

Yet even these are in the last resort phantasmal, the projection on a screen of the ultimate realities. On one side they are sharply set against sorrow and suffering, ill-allied love, human impotence and frailty, the infinite pity of things. On the other they merge in the passionate craving and the glimmering hope for " the further shore," in the mystical doctrine of lives again and again reincarnated, of the drinking of Lethe so that souls " may begin to be willing to return again into bodies," of the renewed labour, the grief, the endless effort, at last, perhaps, and for some, if only for a few, — *pauci laeta arva tenemus* — coming to an end, as the elect are rapt or sublimated into an actual Paradise.

## XI. VIRGIL IN THE MEDIEVAL AND MODERN WORLD

VIRGIL'S fame and his popularity were both established in his own lifetime, and both had a great accession on the publication of the *Aeneid*. He had his detractors,[35] among the small fry of contemporary poetasters, and among the purists or archaists who held obstinately by the older Latin tradition. But his fastidious shyness kept him aloof from literary cliques and from controversy; he was absorbed in his own work; and he had the powerful backing of imperial favour, and the affection of all who, whether statesmen or men of letters, were admitted to his acquaintance. Both fame and popularity came to him of themselves. The *Aeneid* was at once accepted as the great national poem. Copies were rapidly multiplied. It was not only in the hands of every educated man and woman, but became what it has ever since remained, a standard schoolbook for the western world.[36] Knowledge of it spread through all classes;

snatches from it have been found cut on the walls of the public baths in Rome, and scribbled on stucco in the buried streets of Pompeii. The *Eclogues* and *Georgics* had become schoolbooks already in their author's own lifetime. We happen to know where this use began, though we cannot guess where it may end and need not anticipate that it will. It was in an advanced Secondary School for boys of over fifteen opened in Rome in or about the year 26 B.C. by one Q. Caecilius,[37] an Epirot Greek by birth, and a freedman of Atticus, the famous banker and friend of Cicero. Later, a well-known line of Juvenal [38] describes the stained and smeared Virgils that were in the hands of ordinary schoolboys. Martial mentions that a portrait of Virgil was often prefixed to them.

There were reactions, such as happen with all writers, even the greatest, before the world settles down (if it ever does) to a final judgment. Caligula's proposal to expel Virgil from all the public libraries was only the eccentricity of a madman. But later, the great archaistic revival in the age of the Antonines brought the older poets for a while again into favour. Hadrian headed a fashion of "preferring

Ennius." Virgil had been so assiduously copied by poets of the intervening century that, when people grew tired of them, the reputation of Virgil himself had a set-back. It suffered too from the army of grammarians and commentators who were let loose on him; of these there was a continuous series down to the beginning of the Dark Ages. But his prestige and predominance were not substantially impaired. The whole of post-Virgilian Latin literature, in prose as well as in poetry, is saturated with Virgilian quotations, adaptations and allusions, as much as English literature for the last three hundred years has been with Shakespeare, and even more.

Not only so; but his poems, the *Aeneid* especially, became a sort of Bible. The famous *Sortes Vergilianae,* a method of seeking in them for supernatural guidance, came early into vogue. The phrase as well as the thing was already established a century after his death, perhaps sooner. Not only the practice, but a large measure of belief in its efficacy, lingered on into the seventeenth century. Oracles were sought by formal and ritual consultation of the *Aeneid* in temples. It took, for this purpose, the place of the discredited Sibylline Books.

Hadrian, according to his biographer, consulted both, and received from both the prophecy of his future elevation to the principate.[39] Clodius Albinus received his *sors* from two lines of Virgil in the temple of Apollo at Cumae; Alexander Severus his in the temple of Fortune at Praeneste: the great Illyrian Emperor Claudius, towards the end of the third century, "in the Apennines," not only for himself but for his descendants, the Imperial house of Constantine.

Virgil, indeed, was thought of and treated as in some sense deified, and able from the other world to exercise control or intervention in human affairs. His birthday, like that of Augustus, was registered in the Calendar as a saint's day. Poets, like Statius and Silius Italicus,[40] worshipped at his tomb as at a shrine. Alexander Severus placed his bust in the *lararium* or family chapel of the Imperial palace, where divine honours were paid to it. This worship would have ceased with the decay of paganism; but it was taken over by the Christian Church. The *Fourth Eclogue* was accepted and proclaimed as a direct prophecy of the birth of Christ. It was so expounded, in an address to the whole Christian population of the Empire, by Constantine after he had decreed the recognition of Christianity as the State religion.[41] Thenceforth it was taken for granted, and almost became an article of faith. St. Augustine not only accepts this doctrine, but actually cites Virgil's own mention of the Sibylline prophecies — the *Cumaeum carmen* of the *Fourth Eclogue* — as authentic proof of the genuineness and validity of those earlier predictions. In the second childhood of Latin letters, the construction of centos from Virgil was a favourite and elaborate occupation. Masses of these have been preserved. Many were ingeniously forced into a Christian sense, and actually made use of in churches. Pope Gelasius at the end of the fifth century, when making an authoritative revision of the Canon of Holy Scripture, is said — though on the evidence of doubtful documents — to have found it necessary to exclude these from the Canon by name.[42]

Legend after legend was invented on the strength of this belief. St. Paul was said to have visited Virgil's tomb on his way from Puteoli to Rome, and to have wept at the thought that he had died before the Light had come into the world. The story was incorporated in the special office for St. Paul's day at Mantua. In the Christmas Services at Rheims, "Maro, prophet of the Gentiles," was called on with the prophets of the Old Testament to bear witness to Christ. Popular fancies ran into still greater extravagances. Virgil the prophet became Virgil the magician. Round his name grew a mass of fantastic tales, which, originating perhaps at Naples, spread all over Europe. They bulk largely in the *Gesta Romanorum*, the most widely popular of all medieval books. They were the foundation of many romances in prose and verse from the twelfth century onwards. One of these, *Les Faictz merveilleux de Virgille*, passed through edition after edition in the early days of printing in France, and was translated into nearly all the languages of Europe.

Concurrently, among serious scholars, Virgil, while he was admired as a poet, was still more approached and studied as a fountain of philosophy. Already in the fourth century his commentator Donatus, the teacher of St. Jerome, had to begin by insisting that Virgil was a poet and not a professor of metaphysics. He had come to be called the Plato of poets. Many attempts were made — they have been renewed down to our own day — to extract from the mystical pageantry of the Sixth Book of the *Aeneid* a coherent body of scientific and theological doctrine, to assign to Virgil an exact place among schools of thought and framers of systems. They are all futile. Virgil was not an Epicurean or Stoic, a Pythagorean or Platonist. He was not a philosopher in his ideas any more than he was an historian in his narrative; he was a poet.

But poetry, as has been truly said, is the ultimate expression both of philosophy and of history. It not only interprets, but re-creates both; it is already at the centre towards which they are always approaching but which they never reach. "Poetry," writes Arnold, "is the speech in which man comes nearest to being able to utter the truth." But more than that; poetry at its height does utter the truth; and it carries its own conviction. It reaches its height but seldom, in few poets and not always in these. But where it does, its vitality and its vitalizing power are both immortal; a thousand years to it are but as one day. Virgil, as we have seen, was the imaginative interpreter and the spiritual creator of a great ideal, for human life and for the organization of the nation and the world. Thirteen hundred years after his death, that ideal was re-embodied by Dante.

Dante is the culminating figure of the Middle Ages; he is also the creator of modern literature: and Virgil was Dante's acknowledged and adored master. It is under Virgil's direct guidance that he passes through the realms of punishment and the circles of cleansing, only leaving him when he reaches the edge of the final Purgatorial fire. On him he lavishes, in endless profusion, all names of adoring praise. *Savio duca, dolce padre, alto dottore, gran maliscalco, pregio eterno, virtù somma, scorta fida, mar di tutto il senno,* — "sage guide, sweet father, high teacher, grand commander, eternal treasure, supreme virtue, faithful escort, ocean of all wisdom"— these are but a selection from the titles by which Dante names or invokes him. Oftener still he is simply *il poeta,* "the poet": no epithet is needed. From him Dante took, as one torch kindling from another, three things: first, the long-lost *bello stile,* the beauty of language which he regained for European poetry; secondly, the vision of the ordained divine government of the world; thirdly, the prophetic and operative faith in the unity and supremacy of Roman Italy.

The *bello stile* was lost before the Dark Ages descended upon Europe: it was through return to Virgil more than through any other single influence that it was recovered. It has never been quite lost again, but we still have to go back to the fountain-heads to secure it; no later sources give it in all its strength and purity. In Virgil's own land and in Dante's own language, Petrarch and Boccaccio, Ariosto and Tasso, Leopardi and Carducci have all drunk largely of that living water; and no less in the English-speaking race over two continents have Chaucer, Spenser, and Milton; no less have Wordsworth, Shelley, Keats, and those others who since then have borne the lamp of the Muses. Virgil is not only the precursor, but one of the most direct, powerful and continuous sources of the whole splendid body of our poetry from the fourteenth to the twentieth century. As a master, a model, an inspiration, he has not lost and will not lose his virtue.

There may be added here, to reinforce what has been said already as to the vitalizing power of Virgil's genius, and to shew its effects in actual working, some review of the influence which the *Aeneid* has had on the English poets.

That influence has been operative continuously from the first faint beginnings of learning and of national culture. It can be traced expanding through the Middle Ages, the Renaissance, the one hundred and fifty years of the Elizabethan and Stuart reigns, into the classicism of the eighteenth century. That century was a period of classical attainment and of romantic revival. In both, the Virgilian influence was potent. But it is hardly less marked, though now it takes new forms and involves fresh interpretations, in the poetical world opened up by Wordsworth and Coleridge, Shelley and Keats, and explored through the multiform product of the Victorian age, up to the point at which we begin to deal with the work of poets still living. Within the limits of this sketch, it would be impossible to traverse, in the most summary way, so immense a field of history; and equally impossible to pursue the Virgilian influence through its detailed working in a single poet or group of poets. All that can be done is to note some salient points in the long story, and to illustrate it by a few instances which may serve as clues towards appreciating the kind and degree of force which the *Aeneid*, as a living work of art, has exercised and still exercises over our own poetry as a science, an art, and a creative interpretation of life.

Not only for the Middle Ages, but for the succeeding times down to the revolutionary movement which created the modern world, the *Aeneid* was taken for granted as a poem of acknowledged and unquestioned supremacy. Virgil was the Master of the Poets; the *Aeneid* was a model which had to be followed by all poets writing on the grand scale and in the grand manner. "Reed Virgile in Eneidos" is the succinct advice of Chaucer in *The House of Fame;* and to "folwe word for word Virgyle," as he says in *The Legend of Good Women,* was the aim pursued not only as the highest but as an approximately attainable ideal. He might be — indeed he was proclaimed to be — inimitable; but to imitate him as far as possible, to tread in the path which he had once for all laid out, was a mere duty as well as an august privilege. The other masters derived from him, themselves following, with a kindred genius quickened by intense study, the Virgilian cadence and diction, — in Milton's words:

"*Hither, as to their fountain other Stars*
*Repairing, in their golden urns draw light,*
*And hence the morning planet gilds his horns.*"

The great Italian poets, under whose influence English poetry ceased to be insular and took its place fully in the European Republic of Letters, were in a sense but the channel through which the Virgilian inspiration flowed. The European epic, from Boccaccio downwards, was the process towards reconquest of the Virgilian epic. The movement culminated in its last great Italian exponent, Tasso. The *Gierusalemme Liberata* (1581) was a direct model of the highest importance for both Spenser and Milton as well as for lesser English poets; and Tasso's whole work is based on and rooted in the *Aeneid*. His elaborate similes are very often nearly exact reproductions of Virgil's; in whole stanzas, in whole episodes, and these not the least beautiful or least successful portions of his epic, he carried reconstitution of the manner, style and substance of the *Aeneid* to the highest attainable point.

A simpler age had admired, without attempting to regain, Virgil's specific poetical quality: Chaucer, with his outburst of far-off reverence —

*"Glory and honour, Virgil Mantuan,*
*Be to thy name! and I shal as I can*
*Folow thy lantern as thou gost biforn —*

expressed that less ambitious attitude. But when the Revival of Letters touched England, the new poetry turned instinctively to the *Aeneid* for inspiration, finding in it the accomplishment of its own highest aims. Modern English poetry may be said to begin with the Earl of Surrey, "the English Petrarch." It was not merely as a writer of lyrics and sonnets that he opened the way for it. It was still more markedly by his translation of Books II and IV of the *Aeneid*. In it he created, to all intents and purposes, English blank verse, the national vehicle ever since for poetry of epic scope and compass. He gave it the decisive impulse towards becoming a vehicle comparable to the Latin hexameter; and he succeeded in doing so because, by a stroke of genius, he harnessed it to the rigorous task of actually reproducing Virgil, and thus brought the matter to a searching test.

Such also has been from time to time the effort renewed by English poets during the four centuries from Surrey's time to our own.

It is remarkable how many of them have spent labour in translating Virgil, partly as a technical exercise, partly in order to bring themselves more directly within the Virgilian influence and, if it were possible, to discover his secret. These translations are of course only an index-figure to their study of the *Aeneid* and to the more diffused or transmuted Virgilianism which is an element in their own original poetry. But Dryden's translation of the *Aeneid* became, in itself, an English classic. Not only was it a work of genius, but like Pope's *Homer,* it helped to create a standard for English poetry the effects of which are still unexhausted. Still more interesting is it to note the study given to the *Aeneid* and the inspiration derived from it by the Romanticists in their reaction against a sterilized classicism. Wordsworth renews the Virgilian manner, with a deeper and subtler appreciation, in many passages of *The Prelude,* and more notably in the famous *Laodamia;* and his rendering of part of *Aeneid* I into heroic couplets, made just a hundred years ago, shews how strong the Virgilian influence was on him in mature years. Keats, while still a schoolboy or little more, turned the whole *Aeneid* into English for his own satisfaction; and the results of that youthful study may be traced later in *Lamia* and *Hyperion*. Of Matthew Arnold it is almost needless to speak; his celebrated allusion to

> "*the Virgilian cry,*
> T*he sense of tears in mortal things,*"

is but one among his many tributes to the potency of Virgil's art as a living force. Arnold belonged to the classical school and was brought up in the Latin tradition. It is more striking therefore to find the influence of Virgil as potent at the other end of the line. Morris' translation of the *Aeneid* was executed, for pure love of the poet whom he acknowledged as one of his own masters and a supreme master of poetical art, after he had himself won a place, in the fields both of romance and of epic, among the great English poets.

It is of course in Tennyson, of all the English poets of the last century, that the Virgilian influence is most obvious and most pervasive. He has himself borne the most direct and most eloquent witness to it. All readers of poetry throughout the English-speaking world are familiar with the passage in *The Daisy* where he tells us how a phrase of Virgil "kept a ballad-burthen music" in his head for hours upon hours and moulded his own voice to its cadences: with the sonnet in which, with mingled affection and reverence, he enthrones

> "*Old Virgil, who would write ten lines, they say,*
> *At dawn, and lavish all the golden day*
> *To make them wealthier in his readers' eyes,*"

among the heavenly choir whose music is deathless: and above all, with the magnificent lines *To Virgil* written for the nineteenth centenary of the poet's death, which are at once the finest and amplest account ever given of the profound and majestic quality of the *Aeneid*, the fullest acknowledgment of his own lifelong devotion to Virgil, and the nearest approach made by any modern poet to the splendour of the Virgilian verse. But page after page might be filled with citation of passages where he moves in Virgil's footprints and is inspired by his influence. Sometimes this is through direct assimilation and reproduction, as in the early poem *On a Mourner* with its marvellous recollection of *Aeneid* III, 147, following:

"*And when no mortal motion jars*
*The blackness round the tombing sod,*
*Through silence and the trembling stars*
*Comes Faith from tracts no feet have trod,*
*And Virtue, like a household God*

*Promising empire; such as those*
*Once heard at dead of night to greet*
*Troy's wandering prince, so that he rose*
*With sacrifice, while all the fleet*
*Had rest by stony hills of Crete.*"

Sometimes it is in the elaborate harmonies of the epic simile, of which one instance may serve for many:

"*As comes a pillar of electric cloud*
*Flaying the roofs and sucking up the drains,*
*And shadowing down the champaign till it strikes*
*On a wood, and takes, and breaks, and cracks, and splits,*
*And twists the grain with such a roar that Earth*
*Reels, and the herdsmen cry.*"

But far oftener it is in a subtler though not less conscious or less recognizable kinship, as from the *Ulysses* of 1833,

"*Old age hath yet his honour and his toil;*
*Death closes all: but something ere the end,*

*Some work of noble note, may yet be done,*
*Not unbecoming men that strove with Gods,"*

to the invocation of near sixty years later,

"*Spirit, nearing yon dark portal at the limit*
*of thy human state,*
*Fear not thou the hidden purpose of that*
*Power which alone is great,*
*Nor the myriad world, His shadow, nor the silent*
*Opener of the Gate."*

But indeed throughout the whole range of our poetry, the accent and even the phrase of Virgil recurs where the voice of the English poet sounds most fully and melodiously.

In following out this study — one of fascinating interest and of high importance both towards intelligent appreciation of English poetry, towards its practice as an art, and towards the larger study of poetry itself as the highest expression in all ages and languages of human thought and emotion — we must bear in mind that four separate elements in the *Aeneid* have to be traced and weighed. First, there is the epic structure, the large architectural lines of composition on the grand scale. Secondly, there is the ornament, the embellishment of the structure in detail, covering the whole of what may be called the artistic evolution of the poem. Thirdly, there is the rhythm and phrasing which gives poetry its musical value. Fourthly, there is the diction. It is in Milton, and perhaps in Milton alone, that all these four together are absorbed and re-created. The *Paradise Lost* draws from many sources to which Milton's wide reading and profound study gave him access. But of all these, the *Aeneid* takes the foremost place. As regards the first two elements, this is too obvious to require commentary. But no less remarkable is Milton's debt and kinship to Virgil in the incomparable management of periodic rhythmical structure, and in the choice and use of words which create, out of a rigorously restricted vocabulary, a language which in its amplitude, dignity, and precision no less than in its rhetorical quality, is the high-water mark for the art of poetry.

The art of poetry is in continual movement. It follows — and in a very real sense it leads — the movement of life, of which it is the expression and interpretation. Its successive incarnations give place one to another. Lyrical instinct is so grounded in the English genius that it gives to the whole body of English poetry a quality of its own; the epic as such is to some degree foreign to the English mode of creation; and still more is it foreign to the movement which now runs so strongly towards dissolving and democratizing all art. Even in the eighteenth century there was a revolt against it. "Epic poetry," Horace Walpole said, "is the art of being tiresome in verse." But there is no kind of poetry, then or now, on which the same criticism could not be passed. For the enormous and chaotic production of the present age, it is more than ever essential to have a standard of quality, to preserve and study and appreciate the masterpieces. This standard Virgil gives, more fully perhaps than any other single poet. The phrase in which he was characterized three hundred years ago by Bacon still holds true: "The chastest poet and royalest, Virgilius Maro, that to the memory of man is known."

Art is what gives form and meaning, beauty and joy to life; and poetry is the queen of the arts. In the exercise, in its fullest compass, of the art in which he was so great a master, Virgil is not merely an interpreter or expounder, but a creator. He incarnated ideas; he made history. He stands alongside of, and a little above — but how much that little is! — statesmen and thinkers, as joint creator of the Holy Roman Empire which was for centuries the mould and frame of European civilization. That Empire, so far as it ever existed otherwise than as an ideal, has passed away: it became a dream. But Virgil's creative touch did not end with it. He is joint creator of a present and actual ideal, the largest perhaps which has yet been placed before mankind; he is the poet and prophet of no mere League of Nations, but of a single world-commonwealth, and of the fulfilment of the divine purpose in an ordered and universal peace.

The unified and Roman Italy which was Virgil's primary ideal or aim, the one which lay nearest his eyes and his heart, was to some degree, and for a time, realized. Then it broke to pieces, it crumbled and dissolved into vapour, not to reappear in tangible shape for more than a thousand years. In our time it has been reborn. Those are yet living who saw the first creation since a thousand years back of an Italian kingdom; our own days have seen its slow unification, its extension to its natural boundaries, the larger hope of its concord or coalescence with the spiritual power which still lives in the name of Rome. Virgil's vision is, for Italy and for the world, a living inspiration, an aim pursued with unquenchable ardour, a prophecy that brings more and more of its own fulfilment.

We stand now, as Virgil stood, among the wreckage of a world; he can give light and guidance to us in the foundation of a new world upon its ruins. Mankind is, above all, human; what it above all needs, not in education only but in the whole conduct of life, is humanism; consciousness of its own past, faith in its own future, the sense of truth, beauty, joy. This last is the gift of art: art is joy. The human value of all great works of art is not only imperishable but unreplaceable. Virgil is one of the greatest of artists; and it is as such that he finally claims the study which he more than repays, the love which that study increases the further it is pursued and the more largely it is communicated.

## XII. STYLE AND DICTION: THE VIRGILIAN HEXAMETER

VIRGIL'S lifetime covers the period in which the Latin language was perfected as an instrument of expression; and in Virgil himself the technical achievement of Latin poetry admittedly culminates. He had great predecessors, but he carried the art to a point which they had not reached. He had distinguished successors, some of them like Ovid cleverer technicians than himself; but they all count together as his followers, as the post-Virgilians. Fundamentally of course this is because his own poetical genius was so incomparable. But that genius arose just at the time when the technique of the art was, after much laborious effort, on the point of being mastered. He mastered it; and after him, it took no new development.

Apart from a few juvenile exercises, he concentrated wholly on a single metrical vehicle, the dactylic hexameter. This was the metre of the Homeric poems and of another poem not less widely known, read, and learned by heart throughout the Hellenic world, the *Farm-Calendar* (the so-called *Works and Days*) of Hesiod. It was established as the recognized form of verse for all later Greek epics, and for the whole province of philosophic, scientific, or didactic poetry. Theocritus and his school gave it a still further scope, using it not only (with certain subtle modifications of handling) for pastorals, but for the wider field of descriptive sketches, romantic narratives, and epic idyls. In all these directions Latin poetry had followed suit, first by exercises in translating or adapting, then by launching out on original work. Virgil had, together with many others, Ennius, Lucretius and Catullus before him as models and incitements.

It must never be forgotten that the Latin hexameter was a foreign metrical structure. The native rhythm of the Latin language was trochaic; the native forms of verse were accentual, not quantitative. Much the same thing happened with our own poetry. The purely English poetry was composed in verses of an indefinite number of syllables, based on stress-accent and emphasized by alliteration. Equivalence of syllables, and the use of rhymed endings, were both introduced into it from France. The foreign versification was naturalized, after many preludes, by Chaucer. Almost at once it then became dominant; soon it drove the native English type underground, only to reappear as a substantive thing in occasional reversions, but continuing to exercise a great influence over the rhythm and handling of the new poetry; so that English verse is a different thing from French, as Latin verse (though to a rather less extent) is a different thing from Greek.

To adapt Latin to the new rhythm and the quantitative treatment was a very difficult task. Not only did it mean forcing the native rhythms into a new mould; it meant a very serious loss of poetical vocabulary. A Latin poet writing in hexameter was absolutely debarred from the use of many words which were the very staple of his language. Words like *civitas, vigilia, providentia, veritas, contumelia, multitudo, testimonium* cannot be got into hexameter verse at all. With countless words of common and almost necessary use, he was restricted to one or two of their many inflections. He could, to take a few actual instances from Virgil himself, use *imago,* but not *imagines, exercitus* as a nominative, but not as a genitive; he could say *destinat, imprecor, adfert, invideo,* but he could not say *destinavit, imprecatur, adferunt, invidere.* In the first chapter of Livy's History, which gives a rapid sketch of the Aeneas-legend, and in which the general vocabulary, and many of the actual words and phrases, are almost the same as those of the contemporary *Aeneid,* there are, in some fifty lines, twenty-five words which Virgil could not use, besides half a dozen more which he could use only by very awkward elisions. The tendency therefore was for Latin hexameter verse to become cramped, restricted, and monotonously artificial in its diction.

Lucretius had already done miracles with this recalcitrant material. He had by sheer force of genius hammered Latin out into the new mould; he had made the hexameter a vehicle which could and did express close argument, splendid eloquence, thrilling emotion. It remained for Virgil to take the one further step and to transmute this bronze into gold.

He did so, — and in a sense, if we look to what happened to Latin poetry after him, almost too successfully. He exhausted the possibilities of his medium. The artifice, though not the art, of the Virgilian hexameter became the common property of all his successors. Ovid, only a few years later, handles it with amazing adroitness and what seems like effortless ease. But for Virgil himself it remained to the last a matter of perpetual labour and endless experiment. By elaboration of periodic structure, by constant variation of stress and pause, by avoidance of tripping runs and heavy masses, by innumerable verbal or syntactical devices, he made a stubborn material flexible and supple: he gave the language a new music. In this he is like Milton in English poetry. But their methods were different. Milton, debarred by blindness from the help of pen and paper, had to compose *Paradise Lost* in his head and dictated a passage only when he had got it into satisfactory form. Wordsworth, it is interesting to note, did the same thing without the same reason; he did not draft on paper, and when by mental labour that amounted to agony he had got a poem into shape, would make his sister or his wife write it down from his dictation. Virgil, we are told, wrote a first draft and then worked on it until perhaps there was not a word of the first draft left. The *Aeneid* at his death was still full of gaps and stop-gaps, of alternative lines, of passages tentatively cancelled or provisionally inserted, of erasures and interlineations. The editors made, as it seems, no detailed record of what they actually did, whether in choosing between alternative drafts, or in piecing together fragments, or in omitting altogether passages which were unplaced or too obviously incomplete. There are either fifty-five or fifty-six unfinished lines in the *Aeneid* as they published it.[43] But in many other places the substance is incomplete though there is no gap in the metre; there are several paragraphs which seem disconnected, and a few passages which are barely if at all grammatical; there are lines, as well as mere beginnings of lines, which are only rough sketches; there are some metrical inconsistencies; there are tags, sometimes put in to fill a gap, sometimes imperfect provisional solutions of metrical difficulties. It is only by appreciation of this — and such appreciation comes only by long familiarity and minute study — that the genius of Virgil as a master of language can be fully grasped. But it repays the labour. It is a fruitful lesson in the art of poetry.

Almost from the first, Virgil's ear was faultless, his melodiousness exquisite. The progress to be traced in his art is the development of richer harmonies through a larger handling and an ampler movement. The magical single lines of his early work —

> Molli paulatim flavescet campus arista —
>
> Audiit Eurotas iussitque ediscere lauros —
>
> Hic gelidi fontes, hic mollia prata, Lycori —

melt more and more into periods; the music gains more and more of smooth, sweet and rushing freedom. As a masterpiece of full periodic movement, the invocation at the opening of the *Georgics* has never been surpassed. But in his later work at its finest, the art is further sublimated. It even tends to discard the rich ornamentation which is a steady note of Virgil's middle period. In his earlier poetry its use wavers, and his touch on it is uncertain: phrases of almost bald simplicity are mixed with others in which one may feel the decoration to be over-loaded. In the *Georgics* he has fully mastered this among the other problems of technique; and we may say unhesitatingly that both in style and diction he has reached perfection. It would be idle to cite instances when they crowd on the mind so thickly. But later in the *Aeneid* the harmonies become yet more massive, the music yet deeper.

> Ibant obscuri sola sub nocte per umbram
> Perque domos Ditis vacuas et inania regna;
> Quale per incertam lunam sub luce maligna
> Est iter in silvis, ubi caelum condidit umbra
> Iuppiter, et rebus nox abstulit atra colorem.

Beyond this, it might seem impossible for art to go; it might seem impossible to add anything of poise or swell or cadence with the utmost resources of the Latin language in the conquered and perfected hexameter. But Virgil went further. In passages like

Me pulsum patria pelagique extrema sequentem
Fortuna omnipotens et ineluctabile Fatum
His posuere locis, matrisque egere tremenda
Carmentis nymphae monita et deus auctor Apollo:

like

Multae illam frustra Tyrrhena per oppida matres
Optavere nurum; sola contenta Diana
Aeternum telorum et virginitatis amorem
Intemerata colit:

like

> Interea extremo bellator in aequore Turnus
> Palantis sequitur paucos iam segnior atque
> Iam minus atque minus successu laetus equorum.
> Attulit hunc illi caecis terroribus aura
> Commixtum clamorem, arrectasque impulit auris
> Confusae sonus urbis et inlaetabile murmur:

the feet of the verse have become wings, the exquisite mechanism ceases to be a mechanism and flashes into air and fire. In that final perfection and that final imperfection — still to the last reaching out to an infinite progress and an etherealized embodiment — the art of Virgil yields its ultimate secret.

# NOTES AND BIBLIOGRAPHY

# NOTE ON THE SPELLING OF VIRGIL'S NAME

The family name Vergilius or Virgilius seems to have been fairly common both in the Latin and in others of the Italic races. Three at least of the name held important magistracies in the last century of the Republic. The fluctuation between *e* and *i* in spelling no doubt corresponds to an actual difference in pronunciation at different times or by different owners of the name. Republican and early imperial inscriptions invariably give Vergilius; and this is the spelling of the earliest and best MSS. of Virgil, both in titles and in the text of *Georg*. IV. 563, where the poet mentions himself by name. The nickname of Parthenias given him by the Neapolitans in his lifetime shows, however, that the pronunciation, if not the spelling, Virgilius, was also then current; it may have been a provincialism. By the fifth century A.D. it had become prevalent, and established itself in common usage throughout the Middle Ages. In spite of the protests of Politian and other scholars, this usage remained unchanged during the Renaissance and until quite recently: and it is as Virgil, not Vergil, that the poet is familiarly known in all the languages of modern Europe. It would be pedantry to attempt to alter this now; and the English-speaking world will probably continue to speak and write of Virgil, though in their Latin texts they will find him called Vergilius.

# NOTES

1. i. e. The Lucretian Gens was one of the great Roman families, harking back to the time of the famous Lucretia.

2. *Aen.*, X. 163–214.
200 ff. *qui muros matrisque dedit, tibi, Mantua, nomen,*
*Mantua, dives avis; sed non genus omnibus unum:*
*gens illi triplex, populi sub gente quaterni,*
*ipsa caput populis, Tusco de sanguine vires.*

3. Macrobius, V. 2.

4. Propertius, II. 34. 63–66.
*Qui nunc Aeneae Troiani suscitat arma*
*Iactaque Lavinis moenia litoribus.*
*Cedite Romani scriptores, cedite Grai!*
*Nescio quid maius nascitur Iliade.*
Cf. Ovid, *Ars Am.*, III. 337.
*Et profugum Aenean, altae primordia Romae,*
*Quo nullum Latio clarius exstat opus.*

5. This is characteristically Italian and may be compared to the intense expectation and hope, throughout Italy in 1901, for a great Mascagni opera.

6. Cf. Norman W. DeWitt, "Virgil at Naples," in *Classical Philology*, XVII. 104–110 (1922).

7. *Sermonum*, I. 10. 44.
*molle atque facetum*
*Vergilio adnuerunt gaudentes rure Camenae.*

8.. Cf. Tenney Frank, *Vergil, A Biography*, New York, 1922.

9. *Eclogue,* II. 58. "Alas, alas! what wish, poor wretch, has been mine? Madman, I have let in the south wind to my flowers, and boars to my crystal springs!" (Trans. by Fairclough).

10. *Aen.,* IX. 446 ff.

*Fortunati ambo! siquid mea carmina possunt,*
*nulla dies umquam memori vos eximet aevo,*
*dum domus Aeneae Capitoli immobile saxum*
*accolet imperiumque pater Romanus habebit.*

11. This influence will be discussed in another volume in this Library.

12. Cf. Martin Schanz, *Geschichte der Römischen Litteratur,* Munich, 1911; VIII, 2, 1, pp. 86, 107.

13. *Thebais,* XII. 816–817.

*Vive, precor: nec tu divinam Aeneida tenta,*
*Sed longe sequere, et vestigia semper adora.*

14. *Georg.,* III. 40 ff.

*interea Dryadum silvas saltusque sequamur*
*intactos, tua, Maecenas, haud mollia iussa.*
*te sine nil altum mens incohat.*

Cf. Servius' *Vita.*

15. Nichols, J. B. B., Sonnet on the Georgics.

16. *Georg.,* III. 336–338. "Then . . . feed them once more about set of sun, when cool evening allays the air and now the dewy moonlight revives the lawns, and the kingfisher is loud on the shore and the warbler in the thickets." (Trans. by Mackail).

*Georg.,* I. 204–207. "Likewise must we no less regard the star of Arcturus and the days of the Kids and the gleaming Serpent, than they who sailing homeward over windswept seas adventure the Pontic and the straits by Abydus' oyster-beds." (Trans. by Mackail).

17. *Georg.,* III. 46 ff.

18. Quoted by Macrobius, *Sat.,* I. 24. 11.

19. Cf. Elizabeth Nitchie, *Vergil and the English Poets,* pp. 79, 116–118, for a discussion of Dido plays.

20. Donatus, *Vita Vergiliana,* C. 23. *Aeneida prosa prius oratione formatam digestamque in XII libros particulatim componere instituit. . . .*

21. Servius, *Vita:*

> *Augustus vero, ne tantum opus periret,*
> *Tuccam et Varium hac lege iussit emendare*
> *ut superflua demerent, nihil adderent tamen;*
> *unde et semiplenos eius invenimus versiculos,*
> *ut*
>
> *Hic cursus fuit.*

22. St. Augustine, *Confessions,* I. xiii.

23. H. Nettleship, *Vergil,* London, 1879, p. 61.

24. J. Cardinal Newman, *The Grammar of Assent,* London, 1870.

25. Cf. Clifford Herschel Moore, *Pagan Ideas of Immortality during the Early Roman Empire,* Cambridge, 1918.

26. *Aen.,* XI. 110–1. "Do ye ask me peace for the dead slain by the lot of battle? Gladly would I grant it to the living too." (Trans. by Fairclough).

27. *Aen.,* VII. 812–813.

28. *Aen.,* XII. 827.

29. *Aen.,* VIII. 99–100.

> *tecta vident, quae nunc Romana potentia caelo*
> *aequavit; tum res inopes Evandrus habebat.*

30. *Georg.,* II. 532.

31. *Georg.,* II. 500–501.

32. *Georg.,* II. 516–522. "And unceasingly the year lavishes fruit or young of the flock or sheaf of the corn-blade, and loads the furrow and overflows the granary with increase. Winter is come; the Sicyonian berry is crushed in the olive-presses, the swine come home sleek from their acorns, the woodland yields her arbute-clusters, and autumn drops his manifold fruitage, and high up the mellow vintage ripens on the sunny rock." (Trans. by Mackail).

33. *Georg.*, I. 121.

34. *Georg.*, I. 200.

35. Donatus, *Vita Vergiliana,* C. 46. *Asconius Pedianus libro quem contra obtrectatores Vergilii scripsit. . . .*

36. Quintilian, *Inst. Or.*, I. 8. 5. *optime institutum est, ut ab Homero atque Vergilio lectio inciperet, quamquam ad intellegendas eorum virtutes firmiore iudicio opus est.*

37. Suetonius, *De Illustribus Grammaticis,* 16.

38. Juv., VII. 225–227. Cf. Martial, XIV. 186.2.
*Quam brevis immensum cepit membrana Maronem!*
*ipsius et vultus prima tabella gerit.*

39. *Script. hist. Aug.*, (Spartianus) *Hadr.*, II. 8. *Quo quidem tempore, cum sollicitus de imperatoris erga se iudicio, Vergilianas sortes consuleret:*

*Quis procul ille autem ramis insignis olivae*
*Sacra ferens? etc.*

*Sors excidit: quam alii ex Sibyllinis versibus ei provenisse dixerunt.*

40. Plin., *Epp.*, III. 7. 8. (of Silius Italicus) *multum ubique librorum, multum statuarum, multum imaginum, quas non habebat modo, verum etiam venerabatur, Vergili ante omnes, cuius natalem religiosius quam suum celebrabat, Neapoli maxime, ubi monumentum eius adire ut templum solebat.*

41. Constantine, *Oratio ad Sanctos,* C's. 19–21.

42. *Centimetrum de Christo Virgilianis compaginatum Versibus, apocryphum:* Labbé, N., p. 1264. The date of Gelasius' alleged decree is A.D. 494.

43. In one case (*Aen.*, V. 595), this point is uncertain.

# BIBLIOGRAPHY

BOURNE, ELLA, "The Messianic Prophecy in Vergil's Fourth Eclogue," in *The Classical Journal,* XI. 390–400 (1916).

COMPARETTI, D., *Vergil in the Middle Ages* (Translation by E. F. M. Benecke). New York, 1895.

FAIRCLOUGH, H. RUSHTON, *Virgil, with an English Translation,* in *The Loeb Classical Library.* 2 vols. New York, 1918–1920.

GARROD, H. W., "Vergil," in *English Literature and the Classics,* edited by G. S. Gordon. Oxford, 1912.

HADZSITS, GEORGE DEPUE, "Some Vergilian Problems and Recent Vergilian Literature," in *The Classical Weekly,* XV. 106–110, 114–118 (1922).

MACKAIL, J. W., *The Eclogues and Georgics of Virgil,* (Translation). New York, 1915.

MACKAIL, J. W., *The Aeneid,* (Translation). New York, 1908.

MUSTARD, W. P., "Virgil's Georgics and the British Poets," in *The American Journal of Philology,* XXIX. 1–32 (1908).

MUSTARD, W. P., "Tasso's Debt to Vergil," in *The Classical Weekly,* XIII. 115–120 (1920).

MUSTARD, W. P., *Classical Echoes in Tennyson.* New York, 1904; C. 8. *Tennyson and Virgil.*

MUSTARD, W. P., "Tennyson and Virgil," in *The American Journal of Philology,* XX. 186–194 (1899).

NITCHIE, ELIZABETH, *Vergil and the English Poets.* New York, 1919. The author discusses "The Mediaeval Tradition." Vergil and Chaucer, Spenser, Milton, Dryden, Pope, Thomson, Landor, Tennyson and the Victorians.

Oesterlen, Th., *Vergil in Schillers Gedichten, Studien zu Horaz u. Vergil.* Tübingen, 1885.

Royds, T. F., *The Beasts, Birds, and Bees of Virgil.* Oxford, 1918.

Sargeaunt, John, *The Trees, Shrubs, and Plants of Virgil.* Oxford, 1920.

Sills, K. C. M., "Vergil in the Age of Elizabeth," in *The Classical Journal,* VI. 123–131 (1910).

Smith, Kirby Flower, "The Later Tradition of Vergil," in *The Classical Weekly*, IX. 178–182, 185–188 (1916).

Tunison, J. S., *Master Virgil.* The Author of the Aeneid, as he seemed in the Middle Ages. Cincinnati, 1890.

Wendell, Barrett, *The Traditions of European Literature,* From Homer to Dante. New York, 1920.

Williams, Theodore C., *The Aeneid of Virgil* (Translated into English Verse). Boston, 1908.

Williams, Theodore C., *The Georgics and Eclogues of Virgil* (Translated into English Verse). Cambridge, 1915.

Winbolt, S. E., *Latin Hexameter Verse.* London, 1903.

Zappert, Georg, *Virgils Fortleben im Mittelalter.* Vienna, 1851.

CONTRIBUTORS TO THE "OUR DEBT TO GREECE AND ROME FUND," WHOSE GENEROSITY HAS MADE POSSIBLE THE LIBRARY

# Our Debt to Greece and Rome

*Philadelphia*

Dr. Astley P. C. Ashhurst
Thomas G. Ashton
William L. Austin
John C. Bell
Henry H. Bonnell
Jasper Yeates Brinton
George Burnham, Jr.
John Cadwalader
Morris L. Clothier
Miss Clara Comegys
Miss Mary E. Converse
Arthur G. Dickson
William M. Elkins
H. H. Furness, Jr.
Thomas S. Gates
William P. Gest
John Gribbel
Miss M. S. Hinchman
Samuel F. Houston
Charles Edward Ingersoll
John Story Jenks
Alba B. Johnson
Miss Nina Lea
Horatio G. Lloyd
George McFadden
Mrs. John Markoe
J. Willis Martin
Jules E. Mastbaum
J. Vaughan Merrick
David Milne
Effingham B. Morris
William R. Murphy
John S. Newbold
S. Davis Page (*memorial*)
Owen J. Roberts
Joseph G. Rosengarten
Miss Caroline Sinkler
William C. Sproul
John B. Stetson, Jr.
Dr. J. William White (*memorial*)
George D. Widener
Mrs. James D. Winsor
Owen Wister
The Philadelphia Society for the Promotion of Liberal Studies

*Boston*

Oric Bates (*memorial*)
Miss Mary H. Buckingham
Frederick P. Fish
William Amory Gardner
Joseph Clark Hoppin
William Caleb Loring
Miss Ellen F. Mason

*Chicago*

John C. Shaffer
Harold H. Swift
Herbert W. Wolff

*Cincinnati*

Herbert G. French
Charles Phelps Taft

*Cleveland*

Samuel Mather

*Detroit*

John W. Anderson
Dexter M. Ferry, Jr.
Henry G. Sherrard (*memorial*)

*Doylestown, Pennsylvania*

"A Lover of Greece and Rome"

*Kansas City*

Charles Baird

*Lancaster*

William H. Keller

*New York*

"Anonymous"
John Jay Chapman
Otto H. Kahn
Willard V. King
Thomas W. Lamont
Dwight W. Morrow
Mrs. D. W. Morrow
*Senatori Societatis Philosophiae, ϕBK, gratias maximas agimus*
Elihu Root
Mortimer L. Schiff
William Sloane
George W. Wickersham
Miss Nellie C. Williams
And one contributor, who has asked to have his name withheld:
*Maecenas atavis edite regibus,*
*O et praesidium et dulce decus meum*

*Providence*

John Nicholas Brown

*Washington*

The Greek Embassy at Washington, for the Greek Government

Our Debt to Greece and Rome

AUTHORS AND TITLES

# AUTHORS AND TITLES


1. HOMER. *John A. Scott*, Northwestern University.
2. SAPPHO. *David M. Robinson*, The Johns Hopkins University.
3. EURIPIDES. *F. L. Lucas*, King's College, Cambridge.
4. ARISTOPHANES. *Louis E. Lord*, Oberlin College.
5. DEMOSTHENES. *Charles D. Adams*, Dartmouth College.
6. THE POETICS OF ARISTOTLE. *Lane Cooper*, Cornell University.
7. GREEK HISTORIANS.
8. LUCIAN. *Francis G. Allinson*, Brown University.
9. PLAUTUS AND TERENCE. *Gilbert Norwood*, University of Toronto.
10. CICERO AND HIS INFLUENCE. *John C. Rolfe*, University of Pennsylvania.
11. CATULLUS. *Karl P. Harrington*, Wesleyan University.
12. LUCRETIUS AND EPICUREANISM. *George Depue Hadzsits*, University of Pennsylvania.
13. OVID. *Edward Kennard Rand*, Harvard University.
14. HORACE. *Grant Showerman*, University of Wisconsin.
15. VIRGIL. *John William Mackail*, Balliol College, Oxford.
16. SENECA, THE PHILOSOPHER. *Richard Mott Gummere*, The William Penn Charter School.
17. ROMAN HISTORIANS. *Guglielmo Ferrero*, Florence.
18. MARTIAL. *Paul Nixon*, Bowdoin College.
19. PLATONISM. *Alfred Edward Taylor*, University of Edinburgh.
20. ARISTOTELIANISM. *John L. Stocks*, University of Manchester.
21. STOICISM. *Robert Mark Wenley*, University of Michigan.

22. Language and Philology. *Roland G. Kent*, University of Pennsylvania.
23. Aeschylus and Sophocles. *J. T. Sheppard*, King's College, Cambridge.
24. Greek Religion. *Walter Woodburn Hyde*, University of Pennsylvania.
25. Roman Religion. *Gordon J. Laing*, University of Chicago.
26. Mythology. *Jane Ellen Harrison*, Newnham College, Cambridge.
27. Theories Regarding the Immortality of the Soul. *Clifford H. Moore*, Harvard University.
28. Stage Antiquities. *James Turney Allen*, University of California.
29. Greek Politics.
30. Roman Politics. *Frank Frost Abbott*, Princeton University.
31. Roman Law. *Roscoe Pound*, Harvard Law School.
32. Economics and Society.
33. Warfare by Land and Sea. *Eugene S. McCartney*, University of Michigan.
34. The Greek Fathers. *James Marshall Campbell*, The Catholic University of America.
35. Greek Biology and Medicine. *Henry Osborn Taylor*, New York.
36. Mathematics. *David Eugene Smith*, Teachers College, Columbia University.
37. Love of Nature among the Greeks and Romans. *H. R. Fairclough*, Leland Stanford Junior University.
38. Astronomy and Astrology. *Franz Cumont*, Brussels.
39. The Fine Arts. *Arthur Fairbanks*, formerly of the Museum of Fine Arts, Boston.
40. Architecture. *Alfred M. Brooks*, Swarthmore College.
41. Engineering. *Alexander P. Gest*, Rensselaer Polytechnic Institute.

42. Modern Traits in Old Greek Life. *Charles Burton Gulick*, Harvard University.
43. Roman Private Life. *Walton Brooks McDaniel*, University of Pennsylvania.
44. Greek and Roman Folklore. *William Reginald Halliday*, University of Liverpool.
45. Greek and Roman Education. *J. F. Dobson*, University of Bristol.
46. Christian Latin Writers.
47. Roman Poetry and Its Influence upon European Culture. *Paul Shorey*, University of Chicago.
48. Psychology, Ancient and Modern. *G. S. Brett*, University of Toronto.
49. Music.
50. Ancient and Modern Rome. *Rodolfo Lanciani*, Rome.
51. Ancient Writing. *B. L. Ullman*, University of Chicago.
52. Apuleius. *Elizabeth Hazelton Haight*, Vassar College.
53. Greek Rhetoric and Literary Criticism. *W. Rhys Roberts*, Leeds University.
54. Roman Rhetoric and Literary Criticism.
55. Cicero as Philosopher. *Nelson G. McCrea*, Columbia University.